POETRY AT PRESENT

by Charles Williams

the apocryphile press
BERKELEY, CA
www.apocryphile.org

apocryphile press
BERKELEY, CA

Apocryphile Press
1700 Shattuck Ave #81
Berkeley, CA 94709
www.apocryphile.org

First published by Oxford University Press, 1930.
First Apocryphile edition, 2008.

For sale in the USA only. Sales prohibited in the UK.
Printed in the United States of America.

ISBN 1-933993-63-4

TO
R. M. L.
IN GRATITUDE AND
AFFECTION

PREFACE

THIS book is meant as an introduction to the works of certain contemporary poets, for those readers who do not know them, while not being, it is hoped, entirely without interest for those who do.

In the present affluent state of verse, some limitation of choice was necessary. It was made first by taking only those poets who were alive when it was begun—Thomas Hardy has since died; and secondly by limiting it among them to those of whom it might be argued that they have, to however small an extent, enlarged the boundaries of English verse. The discussions to which this decision has given rise have shown conclusively how much the critical judgements of sensitive minds may differ. For such a limitation is more difficult than the usual question: Is Tityrus a good poet? There are very distinguished poets now living whose work is generally admired, but they seem to have created that work not only within the tradition but without affecting the tradition. It is possible that in a hundred years they may be remembered when some of the poets here discussed are forgotten; but even so they are of their own order and are therefore here excluded.

I feel a real apology is due to Mr. Eliot, for whose work I profess a sincere and profound respect, though I fail to understand it. But this state of mind, for reasons suggested in the essay, may not be quite so stupid as it sounds. I could not bear to omit him, but I am sure I have not done him justice.

And yet—justice? Who can do justice to living things? Few poets yet have read anything written on them and not been sadly conscious either that they are less than they hoped or that the writer is duller than they feared. The exact, the immortal, verse may so easily be missed; so lightly the one certain thing overlooked and passed by. Such probable defeat awaits the critic, even the unpretentious critic. Even when he says deferentially, 'I like this poem very much indeed', the poet will say coldly, 'This one, of course, is much better. You have utterly misunderstood my thought, my feeling, and my work.' It seems insufficient, after that, to say, 'Still, this is what you made *me* think and feel'. But, as a matter of fact, he did—they all did. That answer, if inadequate, is at least itself unanswerable.

In order to keep it unanswerable, the work of the poets has been confined to their poetry; other books, novels, or studies in battle, travel, or politics, or sorcery, or criticism have been left on one side. Poetry, and poetry alone, is the present business with the poets. The short bio-bibliographies supplied give (where possible) the main dates of publication, but do not, of course, profess to be complete. The poets have gone on publishing while these comments were at the press; the most important of those new books has been the Poet Laureate's *Testament of Beauty*. Had Wordsworth published the *Prelude* while he held the office, the later poem would have had a rival as a Laureate's work. A first reading of it suggests that, though nothing can be added, there is, fortunately, no need to alter or remove anything here.

My gratitude is due to the friends, at Amen House and elsewhere, who have discussed the essays with me; to Mr. J. G. Wilson (for many kindnesses), and to my wife for providing time in which they could be written.

C. W.

20 Sept. 1929.

CONTENTS

Thomas Hardy	1
Robert Bridges	18
A. E. Housman	30
Rudyard Kipling	40
W. B. Yeats	56
W. H. Davies	70
Walter de la Mare	82
G. K. Chesterton	97
John Masefield	114
Ralph Hodgson	128
Wilfrid Gibson	136
Lascelles Abercrombie	149
T. S. Eliot	163
Edith, Osbert, and Sacheverell Sitwell	175
Robert Graves	194
Edmund Blunden	207

PRELUDE

To the poets named in this book

O you good poets, whatsoe'er you sing
   or in what manner, pardon a little thought
   that went among you, and what thence it brought
here speaks of, even may some new traveller bring
into your common city; *ting-a-ling*
   it sounds—no better—as the slow bus fraught
   with talkers, wisely enlarging upon naught,
stays by each house. Mere traffic, but I cling
to such employment, being bred to verse
   from my first years, making it poetry
   (some held) when two eyes looked their first on me,
doing sometimes better thereafter, sometimes worse,
   now calling out the stopping-places. *Ting*,
   the bell goes. *Who will hear a poet sing?*

THOMAS HARDY

1840–1928. At first (1856–61) he was apprenticed to an ecclesiastical architect, and became prizeman of the Royal Society of British Architects (1863) and of the Architectural Association (1863). In his own words, as he contributed them to *Who's Who*, 'wrote verses 1865–8; gave up verse for prose, 1868–70; but resumed it later'.

In 1871 *Desperate Remedies*, his first novel, was published, and the others followed at intervals of a year or two years until 1897. *Wessex Poems*, his first book of verse, appeared in 1898; *Poems of the Past and Present*, 1901; *Time's Laughingstocks*, 1909; *Satires of Circumstance*, 1914; *Moments of Vision*, 1917; *Late Lyrics*, 1922; *Human Shows*, 1925; complete Poetical Works, 1919. *The Dynasts* appeared—Part I in 1903, Part II 1906, Part III 1908.

THE growth of Thomas Hardy's reputation was less like that of a man than that of a myth. Since the Renascence there have been few figures so famous at once for prose and lyric verse and epic drama, and important, if not in philosophical thought, at least in its poignant, human, and poetic expression. No single poet's verse—except Shakespeare's—is more touched with the common knowledge of humanity than Hardy's; none has wandered more intimately among the sad chances and changes of life than his, or more widely among all sorts and conditions of men; nor does any, from beginning to end, bear so clearly, for better and worse, the mark of one shaping mind. All of it arises from a contemplation at once broad and narrow, prejudiced and yet in no definite place unfairly prejudging, and all of it—which has gained him from reviewers phrases (and he disliked them so much!) on 'the dark gravity of his ideas'—instinct with an intense desire for beauty and joy among men.

Nevertheless there is a tale of, let us say, the mythical Hardy which illuminates the actual. It has been said—'Nature said to Hardy "You shan't be a poet". Hardy said to Nature "I will". And he was.' He was, he is, but why does the fable seem so just? To some extent it might be justified even by the title of the first poem in the *Collected Poems* which is called, in a significant phrase, *The Temporary the All*. As that is allowed to sink into the mind it does its own justifying work and persuades us to be content with it. But at first there does appear something a little grotesque about it; it has an air of having been bullied into place. And indeed only the stoutest admirers of his verse have been able to avoid a suspicion that Hardy does sometimes a little bully his words; he is a little stern with them. If he happens on a word which he found as a noun he will compel it to make itself into a verb if he wishes; he will make six do the work of one, and one do the work of six. He has no pity for the tender things, and yet—apparently in love with so strict a master—they are glad to serve him, they delight to be employed even against their nature, and they will make for him the loveliest little songs directly after he has been compelling them to some intellectual hod-carrying. If an example of this severity were needed it could be found in the same first poem—

Cherish him can I while the true one forthcome...

How strained, how pushed into place 'forthcome' is! It is true these verses are called 'Sapphics' and every one knows it is difficult to write Sapphics in English. But a page or two farther on is a poem called merely *Hap*, and again—unused as we are to seeing the word without its companions 'good'—or 'ill'—it looks a little cold and lonely, a little awkward, standing there in a shivering isolation. But it is ungracious and ungrateful to go on citing instances. One more (of a happier kind) may suffice. In an exquisite song of two stanzas called *Weathers* occurs the line

> And maids come forth sprig-muslin drest.

Probably 'sprig-muslin' was never made into an adverb before, but how delightful and beautiful it is there! what a sufficient sense of growing spring it gives!

The effect of this treatment of words indeed, so marvellous are the ways of the Muse, is to heighten the whole aesthetic satisfaction of Hardy's work. This compulsion is joined with another unpoetic habit of his of using a phrase for a word—and all things work together for good. When in the same first poem he says of a 'damsel' that she was

> Fair, albeit unformed to be all-eclipsing,

one feels at first that he has been harder on her than was necessary. But her feelings have to be neglected; it is precisely that almost prosaic clumsiness which will do Hardy's work for him and us; as in that other poem which begins—

> He lay awake, with a harassed air.

It is not clumsiness, it is Hardy's Muse speaking with her own deliberate meiosis, and it is that meiosis, with its preferred inadequacy, its preferred entanglements, which is one charm of his poetry.

An even more complex mutation takes place with other words. Hardy has not only changed prose into poetry; he has, more surprisingly, changed poetry of one kind into poetry of another. The word 'damsel', for example, is quite definitely a word which carries with it a poetic air: the kind of word which in dictionaries is marked *obs. and poet.* (and could there be a more unfortunate fate for any word?), and which does in fact nowadays seem to be obsoletely poetical. Even a professional poet, so to speak, a poet like Mr. Yeats or Mr. de la Mare, would hardly say 'damsel'. It is barely Tennyson; Scott, perhaps. But Hardy has taken this ageing word and sent her out, quite naturally, into his own world, where, rejuvenated, she trips as lightly as any.

And that world is a world which had not so far existed in English verse, and which it is good should exist. But because the very matter of poetry cannot be re-expressed in prose, because it is not only a dull but a foolish thing to try and re-shape what could only be shaped in that way and in those words, it has to be approached sideways, through what it says to the logical mind. Since, however, Hardy, in the preface to the volume called *Late Lyrics*, has claimed that the real function of poetry is the 'application of ideas to life (in Matthew Arnold's phrase)', and that his own contains such an application (which it certainly does), there need be less hesitation in discussing the ideas. But it ought to be done, not with a detached testing of their philosophical value, but with goodwill towards them and a desire to experience to the full the poetry which they have helped to create.

Two of the titles of his books were *Satires of*

Circumstance and *Moments of Vision*, and these two titles combined might give us Hardy's universe. And if we remember also other titles—*Time's Laughingstocks, Wessex Poems, Human Shows*—they will give a still better suggestion of the range and scope of his sight and insight. Two of them are 'tendencious': they hint at what his universe contains—existences which are mocked by time and circumstance, by nature and man, by the process of things and by the apparent momentary stability which man has created for himself in and out of that process. The word vision provides that world with the sincerity of its hypothesis; for Hardy at any rate things are thus and not otherwise. And tales and lyrics are reminders that at least a not negligible part of his work is merely the expression of experience without a hypothesis—or as much without it as is possible to the thought of man.

The exact relation of experience and hypothesis is a definition impossible, in its nature, to make; yet the need of such a definition has continually hampered the full and proper enjoyment of this verse. On one side stand those poems which are moving expressions of experience, momentary realizations of man's good or evil fortune. On the other are those which, by their order and juxtaposition, force upon us the conviction that Hardy (with as much unconsciousness as can be, no doubt) is a propagandist and—one might almost say, considering the poems in which he introduces the idea of God—a theologian. And with these would go the poems in which he definitely dealt with philosophical ideas, were it not that these, exactly because they deal directly with this hypothesis and make it into poetry, do not leave us to realize it by accident and subject us to a possible reaction against it. Of this only partially concealed propaganda the *Satires of Circumstance* themselves are the best example. There are fifteen of them, all put together, and dealing with moments which suddenly reveal to the various protagonists the detestable irony with which the world mocks at them—the dying man who overhears his wife ordering new clothes soon to be 'required For a widow, of latest fashion'; the Bible-class girl who, after a moving sermon, sees the preacher, 'her idol', re-enacting his pulpit gestures in the vestry mirror 'with a satisfied smile'; the mothers squabbling in a cemetery over the graves in which they suppose their children are buried, when 'we moved the lot some nights ago' to make way for a new main drain; and so on. There is not one of them which is in itself overdone, nor one which is impossible. But man judges the average of chances more wisely than Hardy, it is almost impossible to read those fifteen short poems through at one time without amusement, so pat fall the catastrophes, so victoriously and gloomily are they pointed out. At such times one realizes that even vision may become a habit, but the habit need not blind us to the vision. It would be absurd to say that Hardy has no humour; there is too much evidence to the contrary, and even these satires are obviously intended to have a certain sardonic humour about them. And yet not only here, but in some other poems, one is haunted by a sense that Hardy takes inevitable moods a little too seriously, and omits the normal reaction which is so close as to make part of the mood itself. Every lover at times sees his mistress as something less than ideal, but not every one 'worries' over it quite so much. Every one at times feels that the eternal beauty he remembers and desires and adores is not quite adequately manifested in his particular young lady. But Hardy's lover, riding to meet his lady, meets on the way the true and spiritual 'Well-Beloved', who says,

> proudly, thinning in the gloom,
> 'Though, since troth plight began,
> I have ever stood as bride to groom,
> I wed no mortal man.'

An inevitable truth about love has hardly ever been better put. But this inevitable truth carries with it a perhaps hardly inevitable sequel:

> When I arrived and met my bride
> Her look was pinched and thin,
> As if her soul had shrunk and died,
> And left a waste within.

It is a more than normal imposition of the interior on the exterior, a too individual contemplation of the beloved, a disappointment in happiness rather than love.

Again, in a poem called *At Waking*, a lover sees his lady suddenly robbed of all her charm.

> She seemed but a sample
> Of earth's poor average kind,
> Lit up by no ample
> Enrichments of mien or mind . . .
> Off: it is not true;
> For it cannot be
> That the prize I drew
> Is a blank to me.

It is a perfectly intelligible moment, but so taken

apart from any impulse of laughter or irony, it argues such an utter preceding acceptance of the lady's singularity in 'mien and mind' as to suggest that Hardy was a romantic poet of the first order. This grows to conviction when we reconsider, in the light of the suggestion, the *Satires of Circumstance*, and all those poems which are quite as much satires of circumstance, though they do not come in the group so called—'*Ah, are you digging on my Grave?*' *The Inscription*, *The Duel*, *The Contretemps*, and others. His ingenuity in setting traps for his characters, his unhappiness when they are caught in those traps, his disgust and anger that the process of the world and the traditions of mankind offer no credible purpose and no visible compensation—those things are the marks of a mind wholly abandoned to one idea, a mind desiring perfection and bitterly disappointed at imperfection, a mind not unlike Shelley's in its hunger for the victory of peace and joy in a belligerent and disconsolate world, a romantic mind. But where Shelley satisfied his craving by creating that victory out of his own mind, Hardy has satisfied it by creating out of his own emotional protest a world where all protest is valueless. It is this largeness of creation which has made him so much more than he might at first seem to be.

How has that creation been accomplished? By subdued language, by intense feeling, by a largeness of scope, by the infrequent poems which allow for other moods and chances, by the relation of all to a dominating speculative idea, by the relation of that idea to one of the great critical periods (for us of western Europe) in the history of man. The lyrics and the *Dynasts* form one whole, and the same elements play their part in each division.

A poet's choice of words is obviously dictated by the same spirit that directs his choice of thoughts. But it will not do to assume that the two separate movements unite, or even are parallel, before the central poetic being is found. Hardy's choice of many ordinary and a few extraordinary words, and of some ordinary twisted into extraordinary, moves in his readers' mind the belief that this is a poet who remains close to everyday things; and his mastery of every kind of stanzaic form, his use of many old arrangements and invention of many new, increase that into a willingness to believe that in such common diction and subdued rhythms our daily experiences best express themselves. The tradition of poetry has been to rise at its greatest moments; Hardy's tends to sink. No other poet has been more prosaic when most poetic. There is not in the *Dynasts* a single 'poetic' line, a single line which by its own exalted beauty and power surprises us. Dramatic blank verse has never been so near the rhythm of ordinary conversation. By the subduing of his language almost to the monotone of ordinary life, by the variation of that monotone into a thousand delicate harmonies, by his acquiescence in our normal consciousness, and his multitudinous variations (in the Lyrics) of that consciousness, Hardy creates the illusion of reality which other poets create by their appeal to, and evocation of, our more exalted potentialities of experience. This is the matter of which his universe is made; we recognize and assent to it as being the matter of our own.

He even gives us occasionally an opportunity to compare the two methods. His poem *Without Ceremony* corresponds almost exactly in subject with Coventry Patmore's ode *Departure*. Each is on the death of the poet's wife; each death has been 'without a single kiss or a good-bye'. But compare the first few lines of each poem—

> It was not like your great and gracious ways!
> Do you, that have nought other to lament,
> Never, my Love, repent
> Of how, that July afternoon,
> You went,
> With sudden, unintelligible phrase,
> And frighten'd eye,
> Upon your journey of so many days,
> Without a single kiss, or a good-bye?

That is Patmore's; and Hardy's—

> It was your way, my dear,
> To vanish without a word
> When callers, friends, or kin,
> Had left, and I hastened in
> To rejoin you, as I inferred.

'As I inferred'! 'Inferred'! the circumlocution! the word bullied into its place for the sake of the rhyme! And yet the whole three-stanza poem does not lose its poignancy even by the side of its predecessor.

> And when you'd a mind to career
> Off anywhere—say to town—
> You were all on a sudden gone
> Before I had thought thereon,
> Or noticed your trunks were down.
>
> So, now that you disappear
> For ever in that swift style,

> Your meaning seems to me,
> Just as it used to be:
> 'Good-bye is not worth while!'

Poems of such subdued poignancy—and there are a number of them—do much more than outweigh the invented satires, the 'propagandist' poems; even, in a sense, they justify, or at least excuse, them. They convince the reader that what may appear perversity is no more than the accident which awaits a doctrinal poet—Mr. Chesterton, let us say, as well as Hardy—when he is tempted to speak from his general brief rather than from his immediate experience.

But Hardy, from whichever he may speak, has assisted to enlarge the possibilities of English verse. Unhappy love was, previous to the Victorian age, normally the result of one of two things—unfaithfulness or death; there were other causes, of course, but these were the chief. Hardy has been one of the poets who have most industriously introduced states of mind as causing and expressing distress. The poem *At Waking*, quoted above, is a poem which it would hardly have occurred to any earlier poet to write—except for a realist here and there, my lord Rochester perhaps; and he would have done it so differently that the similarity of the subject would have been concealed. This introduction of a hundred moods and as many ill-chances as the causes of disaster is no doubt partly due to the general inward movement of poetry; it is partly due to Hardy's mere ingenuity in looking for trouble. But it is also partly due to his own intellectual and spiritual sensitiveness; to a mind which, being aware of tragedy as so common and so dreadful, observes, almost involuntarily, how many opportunities for that tragedy present themselves to the unfortunate race of man.

None the less, if all Hardy's poems concluded in a sorrowful or satiric meditation we should feel him to be too unbalanced, too romantic. Fortunately they do not. There are poems of subdued happiness, of real if occasional fun, of a tender wistfulness, of grave but not too sombre recollection. And as we experience these the universe of Hardy's creation becomes more satisfying; extreme romantic though he may be, he at least allows that other provinces than his own exist, and recalls them to us. He has done the same thing in the *Dynasts* by the detachment of the mortals from the Spirits. The rustic scenes, the ball at Carlton House, the concerns of the human protagonists, are allowed to have at any rate an apparent freedom within themselves. When Wellington says

Mon cher Alava, Marmont est perdu,

when the Prince Regent looks anxiously for his wives, when the country folk talk by the beacon, we are, by one means or another, loosened for a moment from the sense of the overruling Idea, and by that very release are the more easily again persuaded of its reality. This is Hardy's poetic skill—over such vast spaces the tyranny of his universe would otherwise defeat itself by appearing too deliberately imposed.

His quietness and poignancy then, his scope and appreciations, are all part of his creative instinct and achievement. But these are variable things; what is the invariable? what is the unity of so many diversities? the philosophical thought that holds them?

He has told us often enough; it is one of the few fundamental ideas about the phenomenal universe possible to man. It is no more entirely convincing in its mere cold existence than any other such idea; like all the rest of them, it holds within itself an 'intolerable antilogy'. All of them need to be loaded with emotion before that element of the grotesque which is bound to exist in them can be accepted or neglected; in that sense Hardy's is no worse and no better than any other. But he has done as a poet what he could not do as a philosopher; he has made the idea convincing by his emotional statement of it and his emotional revolt against it. It is the compulsion that this idea exercises over a poetic genius which seems to detest it that causes us to accept its sincerity and give ourselves up to it in the poetry.

The idea is fundamental and simple. It is in the poem *Hap* (dated 1866)—

> If but some vengeful god would call to me
> From up the sky, and laugh: 'Thou suffering thing,
> Know that thy sorrow is my ecstasy,
> That thy love's loss is my hate's profiting!'
>
> Then would I bear it, clench myself, and die,
> Steeled by the sense of ire unmerited;
> Half-eased in that a Powerfuller than I
> Had willed and meted me the tears I shed.
>
> But not so. How arrives it joy lies slain,
> And why unblooms the best hope ever sown?
> —Crass Casualty obstructs the sun and rain,
> And dicing Time for gladness casts a moan. . . .
> These purblind Doomsters had as readily strown
> Blisses about my pilgrimage as pain:

And in the *Dynasts:*

> In the Foretime, even to the germ of Being,
> Nothing appears of shape to indicate
> That cognizance has marshalled things terrene,
> Or will (such is my thinking) in my span.
> Rather they show that, like a knitter drowsed,
> Whose fingers play in skilled unmindfulness,
> The Will has woven with an absent heed
> Since life first was; and ever will so weave.

But it is not only in the verse of the *Dynasts*, but even more effectively in the prose of the 'stage-directions' that the surprising power of this idea is felt. Everyone knows what the *Dynasts* is—a trilogy, in 19 acts and 133 scenes, dealing with the History of Napoleon and Europe from 1805 till 1815. It is, in two senses, a mental drama—first, it was written for reading and not for stage performance; second, the historical process is set before an audience of mental qualities, personified and dramatized certainly, but remaining abstract throughout—the Pities, the Ironies, the Sinister Spirit, the Spirit of the Years. They correspond to the supernatural powers in the older epics, but, instead of appearing as mortals enlarged and deified, they are frankly our own varying reactions to the history as it unrolls. The Spirit of the Years, the expression of experience and wisdom and knowledge, is the refinement of Hardy's genius into its last observant consciousness. Not only is it he who asserts, against the protests of the Pities, 'still quiring like the young-eyed cherubim', the truth of the Immanent Will, but he has the capacity of presenting existence in its true mode; and the presentation contains some of the greatest sentences that Hardy has written:

> The nether sky opens, and Europe is disclosed as a prone and emaciated figure, the Alps shaping like a backbone, and the branching mountain-chains like ribs, the peninsular plateau of Spain forming a head. Broad and lengthy lowlands stretch from the north of France across Russia like a grey-green garment hemmed by the Ural mountains and the glistening Arctic Ocean.
>
> The point of view then sinks downwards through space and draws near to the surface of the perturbed countries, where the peoples, distressed by events which they did not cause, are seen writhing, crawling, heaving, and vibrating in their various cities and nationalities.
>
> A new and penetrating light descends on the spectacle, enduing men and things with a seeming transparency, and exhibiting as one organism the anatomy of life and movement in all humanity and vitalized matter included in the display.

The largeness of this vision, when combined with the hundreds of single applications of it found in the lyrics, the realism of the language and details, and the intensity of the feeling, are the things that have exalted Hardy to a place higher than that of the mere emotionally-romantic poet. He is one of those few examples of the romantic poet being able so to enlarge his own chosen province as to create from it a universe classic in its effect. There are but two weaknesses in it—the ingenuity of which we have already spoken, and (absurdly enough) its hope. For into that complete and overwhelming universe there intrudes, now and again, a glimmer of another light, of an impossible dream. At the very end of the *Dynasts* the indefatigable Pities suggest

> But—a stirring thrills the air
> Like to sounds of joyance there
> > That the rages
> > Of the ages
> Shall be cancelled, and deliverance offered from the darts that were,
> Consciousness the Will informing, till It fashion all things fair!

Is it irony? or is it 'the unconquerable hope'? If the incident were solitary one would be inclined to think it the first, but it is not. There is at least one beautiful lyric in which the same note is sounded.

This might very well go to confirm the reality of the universe in which it seems to exist, and it may be a matter of individual experience whether it does or not. But to one reader at least it seems to accentuate the romanticism rather than the classicism of the whole work, its admirable and effective partiality rather than its moving and equally effective completeness. This hope is a sign of Hardy's personal revolt against his poetic conviction. And this personal revolt reminds us of the personal ingenuity, the personal abandonment, the personal achievement. It reminds us, that is to say, of romance. No poet of our day has a greater share of that kind of genius than Hardy, and few poets of the past have equalled it. His reputation is assured of permanence, for by him rather than by any other poet the romantic Muse has achieved, without losing her own character, a triumph of classical art.

End Piece

End Piece

He knew the Comic Muse, and made her free
   of seedtime and of harvest, barn and mill;
     and—sole since Shakespeare—with a happy skill
restored her to her wise rusticity:
he knew the large debate of Destiny,
   disputing with itself of its own will,
     and its conclusion in the ominous still
shape and close mouth of loveliest Tragedy.
All the vast movement of the worlds he saw,
   proceeding and returning through the void
     of metaphysic to each dire event:
     Imagination with a deep content
   beholds each crisis fashioned and destroyed
by that unswerving and unresting law.

ROBERT BRIDGES

Born 1844. He took up the study of medicine and became Casualty Physician at St. Bartholomew's, Assist. Physician at the Children's Hospital, and Physician at the G.N. Hospital. In 1882 he retired from medicine and devoted himself to poetry and similar studies. His chief books of undramatic verse are *The Growth of Love* (1876–98), *Eros and Psyche* (1885), *Shorter Poems* (1890, 1894); *Collected Poems* (1899); *Poetical Works* (1912); *October and other Poems* (1920); *New Verse* (1925); *The Testament of Beauty* (1929). He was appointed Poet Laureate in 1913.

OF the fourteen laureates from—and including—Dryden, if we take him as the first, some five (if we include Southey) have been notable poets. With the exception of Dryden himself and of Wordsworth none of them has been a greater than Mr. Robert Bridges. Tennyson is not to be considered a greater, for his verbal achievement is no finer, and his philosophic (if the two can be divided) is very definitely less. None of them has contributed a greater mass of lyric beauty to our literature.

It may very well be held that Mr. Bridges is not only a lyric poet; he has written dramas, a sonnet-sequence, a long narrative poem, and of the volume *New Poems* at least four are more in the nature of philosophic poems than of lyric. But as his lyric verse is more popular, so also it contains so much of intellect that attention may, in such a short tribute as this, be very well concentrated upon it.

Mr. Bridges has been said, by various good judges, to be our greatest lyric poet since Shelley. He was born twenty-two years after Shelley died. But the poetic difference between him and Shelley is immense. There remains something not quite unfair in Matthew Arnold's famous description—'an ineffectual angel beating in the void his luminous wings in vain'. The angel may, merely by virtue of his being an angel, be not entirely ineffectual; the void may be rather an abyss of poetic ether. But Shelley, of all our poets, seems peculiarly unattached to the earth—except in *Œdipus in Thebes* and a few fragments—and peculiarly impatient of intellectual study. A philosophy is to be found in him, but it is not convincing in its poetic intensity. Reason interprets that inspiration too feebly; abstractions become more abstract and aerial and walk less certainly upon our earth.

Mr. Bridges's poetry produces exactly the opposite effect. It is perhaps not without significance that he abandoned a medical career for poetry. For the Laureate is one of the very few living poets who when they speak of abstractions seem to speak of living and significant things. To speak of Beauty, with that capital B, has become almost the defining habit of the minor poet. Mr. de la Mare has dreamed of her, Mr. Abercrombie has cried to her, each convincingly. But neither of these poets has spoken with more assured quietness or with more certain knowledge than Mr. Bridges; neither of them more persuades the reader of the real existence of that Beauty.

And what is true of Beauty is true also of those other abstractions—Virtue, Honour, Truth. What has given to Mr. Bridges's verse this singular prerogative?

Two things—which are indeed one: the concrete instances of these abstractions which he has given us in so many places, and the general quality of his verse.

To give examples of the first would necessitate continued and lengthy quotation. They are to be found in every anthology; they include the famous *London Snow, Asian Birds,* and such poems.

But it is not beauty—of landscape or human figure or great poetry or other art, 'the Virgilian muse' or 'the gaiety of Mozart'—that furnishes the chief hidden theme of this verse, nor is it beauty (merely so undefined) that is its peculiar quality. It is rather beauty in restraint; still more it is the strength of beauty in restraint; or, to press it one farther step, it is the consciousness of the strength of beauty in restraint. Dull as the phrase is, and unworthy to approach the high loveliness of this Muse, all four terms could be justified.

The deliberate act by which Mr. Bridges laid aside the profession of medicine for (what to him must have seemed) the equally arduous profession of poetry was a symbol of his general approach to poetry in all its ways. The deliberate and learned interest which he has taken in the manners and habits of prosody, in the Society for Pure English, in handwriting and phonetics, continue to express that approach. His mind seems to know all the time what it is doing; it judges seriously, if lightly; it is aware of its rejections as well as of its acceptances, even when those rejections appear so natural that almost any other poet would have forgotten them altogether, or perhaps been hardly aware that they existed. Joy, for example, which, in so many poets, seems but an accident of their mood, is here a conscious choice, almost a duty, and even, sometimes, an effort. That some of the finest of his lyrics rise into an attitude of pure delight is no contradiction of this; rather, it is its reward. 'Man's duty is to be happy,' said Dr. Johnson; Mr. Bridges's verse might almost be said to have fulfilled that duty after many a conflict and in spite of many an adversary. That it had an original leaning that way is to say no more than that Mr. Hardy's has had a leaning towards a thwarted happiness or Mr. Kipling's towards a fatalistic morality. But Mr. Bridges omits the consideration of evil fortune less than Hardy omits the consideration of good fortune. 'The master Reason' rides always on the right hand of his Muse when she goes through the cruel habitations of the earth, and directs her attentive glance not only to them but also to the satisfying stars. That the stars have been by now a little touched by the literary taint makes the metaphor only the more just. For a great deal of the happiness in this poetry arises from the recollection of great art.

> Days that the thought of grief refuse,
> Days that are one with human art,
> Worthy of the Virgilian muse,
> Fit for the gaiety of Mozart—

these are the terms in which he praises the 'brighter days' of the sea in one poem; and in another (*Dejection*) he warns his soul, 'revolving hopeless strife,

> Pointing at hindrance, and the bare
> Painful escapes of fitful life . . .

> 'O soul, be patient: thou shalt find
> A little matter mend all this;
> Some strain of music to thy mind,
> Some praise for skill not spent amiss.'

But this too, since literature nowadays is never unselfconscious, accentuates the inward and retired deliberation of this admirable verse. However frequent, however exact, the delight in external things may be, it is within that such delight justifies itself by reason and virtue.

This deliberation accentuates the momentary nature of Joy which is in certain of the lyrics so intensely expressed.

> Haste on, my joys! your treasure lies
> In swift, unceasing flight.
> O haste, for while your beauty flies
> I seize your full delight.

Poets enough have lamented a fugitive joy; not many have realized, as Mr. Bridges has done, that such a flight is indeed (in our present mode of being) of its very nature—that, without it, Joy apparently could not be at all. To such a dogma speculation can offer objections enough; it is, beyond all speculation, confirmed by experience. And it is from profound experience that this verse arises. In a great poem (No. 13 of the *Shorter Poems*, Book III) the gospel, and almost the mysticism, of Joy is expressed.

> Joy, sweetest lifeborn joy, where dost thou dwell?
> Upon the formless moments of our being
> Flitting, to mock the ear that heareth well,
> To escape the trainèd eye that strains in seeing,
> Or home in our creations, to withstand
> Black-wingèd death, that slays the making hand?
>
> The making mind, that must untimely perish
> Amidst its work which time may not destroy,
> The beauteous forms which man shall love to cherish,
> The glorious songs that combat earth's annoy?

Thou dost dwell here, I know, divinest Joy:
But they who built thy towers fair and strong,
Of all that toil, feel most of care and wrong.

Sense is so tender, O and hope so high,
That common pleasures mock their hope and sense;
And swifter than doth lightning from the sky
The ecstasy they pine for flashes hence,
Leaving the darkness and the woe immense,
Wherewith it seems no thread of life was woven,
Nor doth the track remain where once 'twas cloven.

And heaven and all the stable elements
That guard God's purpose mock us, though the mind
Be spent in searching: for his old intents
We see were never for our joy designed:
They shine as doth the bright sun on the blind,
Or like his pensioned stars, that hymn above
His praise, but not toward us, that God is Love.

For who so well hath wooed the maiden hours
As quite to have won the worth of their rich show,
To rob the night of mystery, or the flowers
Of their sweet delicacy ere they go?
Nay, even the dear occasion when we know,
We miss the joy, and on the gliding day
The special glories float and pass away.

Only life's common plod: still to repair
The body and the thing which perisheth:
The soil, the smutch, the toil and ache and wear,
The grinding enginry of blood and breath,
Pain's random darts, the heartless spade of death;
All is but grief, and heavily we call
On the last terror for the end of all.

Then comes the happy moment: not a stir
In any tree, no portent in the sky:

The morn doth neither hasten nor defer,
The morrow hath no name to call it by,
But life and joy are one,—we know not why,—
As though our very blood long breathless lain
Had tasted of the breath of God again.

And having tasted it I speak of it,
And praise him thinking how I trembled then
When his touch strengthened me, as now I sit
In wonder, reaching out beyond my ken,
Reaching to turn the day back, and my pen
Urging to tell a tale which told would seem
The witless phantasy of them that dream.

But O most blessèd truth, for truth thou art,
Abide thou with me till my life shall end.
Divinity hath surely touched my heart;
I have possessed more joy than earth can lend:
I may attain what time shall never spend.
Only let not my duller days destroy
The memory of thy witness and my joy.

But Joy, so desired, so experienced, so hoped, is not his only subject, or rather it has another name, and that name was given it in the title of his early sonnet-sequence, *The Growth of Love*. Within that sequence are contained many implicit or explicit declarations of his temperament, his will, and his aim: for example, the lines—

> Nor surer am I water hath the skill
> To quench my thirst

is almost a definition, by its sound and simile, of his own verse—so cool, so simple, is it. So also the fifteenth sonnet may be quoted here because it seems to describe so well the sort of mind which the reader may conjecture lies behind that verse.

> Who builds a ship must first lay down the keel
> Of health, whereto the ribs of mirth are wed:
> And knit, with beams and knees of strength, a bed
> For decks of purity, her floor and ceil.
> Upon her masts, Adventure, Pride, and Zeal,
> To fortune's wind the sails of purpose spread:
> And at the prow make figured maidenhead
> O'erride the seas and answer to the wheel.
>
> And let him deep in memory's hold have stor'd
> Water of Helicon: and let him fit
> The needle that doth true with heaven accord:
> Then bid her crew, love, diligence and wit
> With justice, courage, temperance come aboard,
> And at her helm the master reason sit.

Love, diligence, wit, justice, courage, temperance, reason—these are the qualities Mr. Bridges praises and recommends to the young adventurer. They are, transmuted into poetry, the qualities of his verse; they are the analysed elements of its beauty as it praises Beauty. They are the method of his experience, and the things his genius chooses to experience are selected by them. Besides great art, a few things are pre-eminent in his poetic knowledge—the English landscape, man in society, Hellenism, solitude, piety. These things, communicated by those virtuous Pleiades named above, cause a profound and still delight. But it is a delight which may require a certain similarity of temperament or a certain prolonged discipline before it can be accepted, especially from a reader used to more violent effects. Violence attends on the steps of a number of our poets, and, so long as it is only allowed to act at its master's bidding, even violence may have its work to do. But it is an uncertain slave, and one whom Mr. Bridges would never spend a farthing to buy or shelter.

One of the best examples of his peculiar strength is in one of the finest love poems of the last century. *Awake, my heart, to be loved: awake, awake—*

> Awake, the land is scattered with light, and see,
> Uncanopied sleep is flying from field and tree:
> And blossoming boughs of April in laughter shake;
> Awake, O heart, to be loved, awake, awake!

The stanza is carried on its wide and awakening vowels. How many poets have welcomed morning in their love-songs, but never before had we seen how, in that world which is neither wholly mental nor wholly actual, being poetry's, never before had we known that sleep fled being uncanopied, nor how, among the new shadows, light is flung over the land, nor felt all this as a simile of awakening and hastening love. 'Uncanopied' is one of the most unusual epithets Mr. Bridges's temperance allows him; as a general rule his adjectives are as near the expected as a poet's could be. But they are always there to do their business, never from mere idleness or the needs of the line. 'Sunny hair', 'stout roots', 'branchèd trees', 'red roofs', 'whirling snow', 'delicious notes', these descriptions are there precisely because it is those separate facts which make beautiful whatever it is we see.

His diction, his feeling for words, is a part of his whole 'duteous chastity'; their potentiality in his verse is that rather of putting off their secular inheritance than expressing it. They mean what they say; that they mean no more than they say is a part of their exquisite simplicity. They are therefore peculiarly fit to convey those landscapes which are so distinct a part of this verse, the visions of 'England in the peace and delight of her glory'. No month of all the year is alien, nor is it easy to say that any month is a more welcome guest to this full-hearted host than any other.

But 'uncanopied sleep' has to fly from our minds yet more completely than in a recognition of the just diction of passionate love or sensitive country-side if we are to appreciate Mr. Bridges's verse properly. It is a marvellous training for the ear. This is no place to discuss his classical prosody, his book on Milton's prosody, or his scazons; they would form a too specialist dispute. But poem after poem in the *Shorter Poems* contains the most delicate rhythms, the most exquisite play of pauses, stresses, and variations. His sonnets, for a gross example, are not poems more or less accommodated to fourteen lines; they are sonnets. In them, perhaps more evidently than in the lyrics, the various long traditions of English verse are to be recognized. It is an additional pleasure to discern, for example, how the metaphysical note sounds in Mr. Bridges's own peculiar harmony; how, instead of that manner issuing in a complex and heightened darkness, it becomes a quiet and heightened lucidity. It is a quiet which is almost too profound for most of us to reach or trust. One sonnet begins

> For beauty being the best of all we know,

and it is in the implicit challenge offered by such a

line to all the easy talk and cheap professions of beauty which go so much abroad in the world that Mr. Bridges's admirers find their own admiration challenged. It will not do, for all its quietness, to take this verse too lightly. It satisfies but it also inquires; its repose is as militant as (it is known) Mr. Bridges can, on occasion, be. No poetry of our day is less pretentious in its doctrine; none is more profoundly doctrinal in its very being. Beauty and love and joy and the rest are here certainly states of existence, but they are also virtues. If the poetry goes often in silver, it is the silver of a natural sanctity, the reward of a persevering and industrious faith. It is as if the genius of Mr. Bridges had determined to know all things in beauty, and as if beauty, here discovered and there imposed, had at last reconciled him to all things.

> Ah heavenly joy! But who hath ever heard,
> Who hath seen joy, or who shall ever find
> Joy's language? There is neither speech nor word;
> Nought but itself to teach it to mankind.

Well, perhaps not. But this voice at least might persuade many minds to be still and wait for the full revelation.

End Piece

End Piece

Sunlight and clear air; the clear air of night—
   is this then the air of earth or heaven, this joy,
   strength with no vehemence, sweetness with no cloy,
but the very sweetness climbing an airy height,
taking again therefrom its heartening flight
   to us whom, hearing that strain, the world's annoy
   may vex with invasion but never so destroy
as that such gay everlasting new delight
dwells not within our minds, 'mid the sanctities
   which Imagination hath for the outer form
     of wisdom made; there paces a courteous Muse,
      her mouth discreet, her brow smooth with the news
   of earth's storm subdued and heaven without a storm,
strong-minded, strong-hearted, healthfully so at ease.

A. E. HOUSMAN

Born 1859. After a Civil Service career of ten years in the Patent Office, he became Professor of Latin at University College, London, in 1892, and in 1911 Professor of Latin at Cambridge. He has edited Manilius and Juvenal. His two books of English verse were published in 1896 (*A Shropshire Lad*) and 1922 (*Last Poems*).

WHEN Mr. Housman wrote the lines

> Therefore, since the world has still
> Much good, but much less good than ill,

he recorded not only his own but also Hardy's vision of this world. But the temper with which his verse has expressed that vision, continuously and epigrammatically, is very different from Hardy's. The revolt and distress which exist in the older poet's work are not to be found either in *A Shropshire Lad* or in *Last Poems*. The two books contain altogether 104 lyrics, with a prefatory paraphrase to the second from Théodore de Banville. No living poet has presented work of such small extent, such unvarying perfection, such renewed intensity, and such catastrophic despair. The illusion, the dream, the desire that things ought to be different, have here no place. Mr. Housman has invented no god to blame; he has, it seems, left behind, so far as man can, even the wish for happiness. Perfect in word, perfect in spirit, these poems arise from a depth of bitter resignation which has not hitherto found expression in English verse. There have been cries of romantic personal despair, but this verse is classic in its restraint and calm balance.

Not that every poem is explicitly concerned with the 'much less good than ill'. A reader who opened *A Shropshire Lad* at the beginning could read the

first sixteen poems without finding in it more than
an occasional stanza of darkness, and without neces-
sarily holding it to be more than dramatic or semi-
dramatic. For those sixteen contain love-songs, a
ballad lyric, and one or two as exquisite nature-poems
as any in English, especially the famous 'Loveliest
of trees, the cherry now' which ends

> And since to look at things in bloom
> Fifty springs are little room,
> About the woodlands I will go
> To see the cherry hung with snow.

This satisfying stanza might have been written
by a young romantic poet; the sense of death is used
as it is used in Nash's 'Queens have died young and
fair'; it seems to be allied to Romeo's great outcry
and Keats's 'cease upon the midnight with no pain'.
It is only in the seventeenth poem that there certainly
enters another style of verse, where the young
cricketer mocks at his own occupation—

> See the son of grief at cricket
> Trying to be glad.
>
> Try I will; no harm in trying.
> Wonder 'tis how little mirth
> Keeps the bones of man from lying
> On the bed of earth.

Grief is here no longer a delicious mood accen-
tuating the contemplation of beauty, but the natural
state of man from which he is tempted to escape by
death. And as the reader passes on he finds that this
state is the one in which Mr. Housman's imagination
normally perceives man to be, but that grief is too
small a name for it. It has no cause, for any momen-

tary cause to which it might be attributed is less than itself.

> The troubles of our proud and angry dust
> Are from eternity and shall not fail.

Here are poems enough on broken or thwarted love, of man for woman or of man for man; enough on parting, and the life and death of soldiers; enough on those who in the past or present are put to death by their fellows. To explain all these things Mr. Hardy has recourse to a metaphysic, but Mr. Housman will have nothing to do with any such attempt to ease the intellect. Mr. Hardy has invented or borrowed a god to argue with; Mr. Housman dismisses the First Cause in a line—'whatever brute or blackguard made the world'. Some laws, it seems, that First Cause has made; some laws, certainly, man. And these laws, if we can, we had better keep.

> How am I to face the odds
> Of man's bedevilment and God's?
> I, a stranger and afraid
> In the world I never made.

The motive is not really cowardice; it is rather that since we can do no better we had better do that.

It is inevitable that, with such a theme, and with certain poems which are a direct encouragement to suicide, the question of suicide should be raised. The business of a poet, of course, anyhow of a poet of a certain kind, is to express his imagination of the universe. Whether that imagination has any practical effect on our lives, and if so what, is a question for us and not for him, and it is an impertinence for us to inquire what effect it has had on his own. Nor is it to be overlooked that by the varying subjects and varying moods of and in which these poems are written, Mr. Housman has created almost everywhere a semi-dramatic effect. But if a poet has given us an harmonious imagination of life it is all the more satisfactory if a mere intellectual question arising out of it can be shown to be answered by its very nature. If we ask these two small books, 'But why should a man go on living?' an answer is there; there are several answers. The first is that, though life is an enemy, death is also an enemy. The exquisite sense of beauty, expressed in the highest form of traditional poetry, is too dear to be parted with—'the cherry hung with snow,' 'the silver sail of dawn',

> The Sun at noon to higher air
> Unharnessing the silver Pair
> That late before his chariot swam,

and so on.

> Could man be drunk for ever
> With liquor, love, and fights—

but he can be drunk so long with such love that only in the very last crisis will he give up the indulgence, though he pays for it in his sober moments. Secondly, if those sober moments are too agonizing he will, anyhow, end them. It is the old undeniable answer— nothing is intolerable, for when indeed things are intolerable we die, either by our own will or against it.

The third and fourth answers are so much in the very heart of this verse that it is ridiculous to speak of them as 'answers' at all. They go before the question; they prevent it being asked; they are part of the nature of things which the verse is marvellously expressing. But in so far as they can be spoken of separately, the third answer is that we go on because we have to go on. Call it self-preservation, call it duty, call it what you will when a name for it is demanded, part of man's very burden is that he is so intensely alive that he is reluctant to cease. 'The troubles of our proud and angry dust' are not quite intolerable; 'bear them we can, and if we can we must'. We cannot die until we can, and when we can we do. Man has become conscious of his nature, and this is his nature. He lives, not from self-preservation or from moral duty, but from something more profound which he only knows because it is himself.

The last answer, put crudely and impossibly, is friendship. Friendship has not been praised so highly as it should have been; of this dearest mitigation of human existence the great poets seem to have been careless in their verse. Perhaps the long preoccupation with romantic and sexual love has caused its serener satisfaction to be neglected, even when it accompanies and is part of that other love. But Mr. Housman, who has no concern for romantic love except as a keen and often thwarted delight, has restored the love between friends to something approaching its right place. When the two books have been read this is left in the mind as the chief satisfaction, the most enduring peace of man. That many of the poems are on exile from friends—either by death or absence—makes no difference. The first poem in the *Shropshire Lad* is on the companionship of men of the same regiment; the last poem in *Last Poems* is on the communal dance at evening on the village green 'at Abdon under Clu'. Between them many of the 104 poems look to the love between friends as their subject or speak of it in their phrases. But perhaps that of all which prints it most clearly on the reader's mind is the poem called *Hell-Gate*. There the poet, with the devil by his side, approaches the gate of hell, where sit Death and Sin, and 'the damned in turn Pace for sentinel and burn'. When they come near

> the sentry turned his head,
> Looked, and knew me, and was Ned.

Recognizing his friend, the sentinel straddles across the way lest he should enter.

> But across the entry barred
> Straddled the revolted guard,
> Weaponed and accoutred well
> From the arsenals of hell;
> And beside him, sick and white,
> Sin to left and Death to right
> Turned a countenance of fear
> On the flaming mutineer.
> Over us the darkness bowed,
> And the anger in the cloud
> Clenched the lightning for the stroke;
> But the traitor musket spoke.
>
> And the hollowness of hell
> Sounded as its master fell,
> And the mourning echo rolled
> Ruin through his kingdom old.
> Tyranny and terror flown
> Left a pair of friends alone,
> And beneath the nether sky
> All that stirred was he and I.

>   Silent, nothing found to say,
> We began the backward way;
> And the ebbing lustre died
> From the soldier at my side,
> As in all his spruce attire
> Failed the everlasting fire.
> Midmost of the homeward track
> Once we listened and looked back;
> But the city, dusk and mute,
> Slept, and there was no pursuit.

It is the strangest and one of the finest of Mr. Housman's poems: strange because in some ways it is so unlike him—with its old mythology and its entire peace, and in some ways so like him, with its colloquial and convincing phrases. Many things have been said at hell gate since Dante and Milton passed there, but few phrases are so satisfying as that of this newcomer; to Sin's smile

> 'Met again, my lass', said I.

It is as great in its way as Farinata in his burning tomb.

And this leads to the manner of Mr. Housman's verse. Of all our modern poets perhaps he and Mr. Yeats alone can manage so well what may be called 'the traditional-poetic' and the 'colloquial-poetic'. But not even Mr. Yeats has used them in such close connexion, and given us therefore an additional aesthetic delight. It would be easy to spoil a poem in the traditional style by using a phrase of modern slang in it; and easy enough to spoil a poem in modern slang by an injudicious attempt to mingle with it lines or stanzas of traditional beauty. But to mingle the two styles so that neither is out of place and that the whole achieves its poetic effect—this is a rarer thing and a triumph, and this Mr. Housman has done. Take, for example, the following poem:

> The fairies break their dances
> And leave the printed lawn,
> And up from India glances
> The silver sail of dawn.
>
> The candles burn their sockets,
> The blinds let through the day,
> The young man feels his pockets
> And wonders what's to pay.

It might be held that the word 'candles' is the one which permits of the transmutation; for this, both by its own nature and by its associations, is allied to both manners. 'Night's candles are burnt out' and 'a pound of candles'—these are the two worlds of speech which are here united. The poem is an example also of the way in which that whole region of faerie and beauty and romanticism is brought into harmony with the controlling idea. For it does not (and this is the distinction of the poem) lose its own value; it remains part of the loveliness which is the temptation to and strength of life.

But if Mr. Housman can do this, and add to his persuasiveness by it, that persuasiveness is due, partly at any rate, to another characteristic of his style—his extraordinary directness. Few poets are so sparing of their inversions; stanza after stanza will run on almost as if it were written in prose. This directness can be observed in the passages that have been quoted, or in

> These are not in plight to bear,
> If they would, another's care.

> They have enough as 'tis: I see
> In many an eye that measures me
> The mortal sickness of a mind
> Too unhappy to be kind.

How slight are the variations from direct speech there! And where they occur they never suggest themselves as coming merely for the convenience of the verse. Questioned and considered, they may nevertheless admit that such a technical convenience was at least a part of the reason for their existence, but it is normally the emotion alone which seems to control the place of every word. Doubtless this is what should happen with all poets, but doubtless also it does not. Inversion so soon becomes a trick, and the writer adds it to the little store of gadgets which help him to shape a poem—the easy adjective, the convenient rhyme, the superfluous phrase. Mr. Housman keeps his poems as free from superfluity as Landor's. There is a kind of poetic innocence about them, a virginity of behaviour which increases the intensity of the message they bring. Their lack of decoration combines with their lack of metaphysic to leave on the reader the impression of a single hard curve down to death. Blake would have hated Mr. Housman's design, but he would have loved its edge.

> O never fear, man, naught's to dread,
> Look not left nor right:
> In all the endless road you tread
> There's nothing but the night.

So completely does such a stanza persuade the reader that he accepts it in every way as final, though (intelligently) he knows it isn't. Even Mr. Housman perhaps derives a little pleasure from editing Latin poets. But that signifies nothing, any more than the similar fact that if this particular poem is part of that night, then it is—so far—an extremely enjoyable night. But against that objection, as has been said, Mr. Housman has provided. *Something* keeps the man treading that endless road through the night, and, whatever it may be, the satisfaction communicated by these poems is a part of it.

End Piece

Night, and the wisdom of eternal loss,
    and down the straight road, far as I can spy,
    a form goes plodding, and that form is I,
a fated stone that cannot gather moss.

But faintly through the darkness he hears come
    the echo of another's feet, and squares
    his shoulders 'neath the burden that he bears,
steps out—and empty is the dark and dumb.

RUDYARD KIPLING

Born in Bombay, 1865; educated at the United Services College, Westward Ho, North Devon. He wrote for Anglo-Indian periodicals, 1882–9; his first book being *Departmental Ditties*, 1886. This was followed by the thin prose volumes—published in India—which made him famous, and later by more poetry: *Barrack Room Ballads* in 1892, *The Seven Seas*, 1896, and *The Five Nations*, 1903. His other poetry has generally been scattered through his prose books, but in two volumes—*Songs from Books*, 1913, and *The Years Between*, 1918—these were collected. A complete edition of the verse to date was first published in 1919. In 1907 he was awarded the Nobel Prize for literature, and the Universities of Durham, Oxford, Cambridge, Edinburgh, Paris, Strasbourg, and Athens have conferred degrees upon him. He was Rector of the University of St. Andrews 1922–5.

Almost all the poets considered in this book have some sort of relation in their work to our general methods of existence. Some of them, and those among the most important, have adopted an hypothesis on which they base a decision on life, a judgement or criticism of it as a whole. Mr. Kipling is apparently an exception. It is not that he fails to instruct us how to live; he does that oftener than more metaphysical poets. He is our great moralist. His verses, 'embellished with the *argot* of the Upper Fourth Remove', preach the doctrines of that inarticulate Upper Fourth to the rest of society. Is this an enlargement of English verse? Did the Muse of Tourneur and Marvell and Johnson and Landor—to say nothing of greater poets—need to know this other language also? And can there be any valuable meaning of which it is the foreordained expression? At first thought, it would seem not.

Yet, as much as with any other of these poets, lines and stanzas of his remain in the memory when the book is closed. Sometimes pleasing, sometimes irritating, they pursue us with a fantastic recurrence. But this is the kind of thing that only happens with distinguished poets. Is Mr. Kipling, then, a distinguished poet?

It seems as if the answer to both these questions must be a combination of two. Our verse had needed Mr. Kipling and yet he is not a distinguished poet; or alternatively we had not needed him and yet he is. The populace know him, and so (sometimes in spite of themselves) do the intelligentsia. It is not enough to say that he sometimes writes badly; all poets do that—except Mr. Housman. Consider Hardy's

> Where are we? And why are we where we are?

Consider Mr. Chesterton's

> And our hope is as far as the firedrake swings,
> And our peace is put in impossible things,
> Where crashed and thundered unthinkable wings
> Round an incredible star.

Even Mr. Yeats, even Mr. Abercrombie, occasionally shoot an arrow awry. But Mr. Kipling seems to be writing best when he is writing worst, which is why he leaves us in confusion, and why the *bourgeoisie* of verse cannot deal with him. He cannot be forgotten and yet he cannot be endured. The Muse corrects with him her own conventions. For even the English Muse, with Keats and Coleridge in her train, has to remind herself that

> There are nine-and-sixty ways of constructing tribal lays,
> And every single one of them is right.

'Tribal lays' is of course capable of two meanings: it may mean lays after the manner of the tribe or lays in praise or exhortation of the tribe. Of the second Mr. Kipling has been justly accused often enough. He will talk of England in a way that destroys all England's greatness, and makes her seem always what she has only sometimes been—one of a horde of semi-barbarians fighting for the richest pasture. But it is difficult to read him without feeling that he also is part of the greatness he has forgotten. For the poems in which England is booted to her place among the nations are interspersed with others in which man becomes more important even than an Englishman. Mr. Max Beerbohm created a marvellous cartoon of 'Mr. Rudyard Kipling takes 'is gal Britannia out'. But on other evenings, when Britannia is engaged and Mr. Kipling is alone, he remembers the East and all the myriad generations, and speaks of them simply and poignantly.

> Pray, brothers, pray, but to no earthly King—
>   Lift up your hands above the blighted grain,
> Look westward—if they please, the Gods shall bring
>   Their mercy with the rain.

Or in *The Mother-Lodge*

> I wish that I might see them,
>   My Brethren black an' brown,
> With the trichies smellin' pleasant
>   An' the *hog-darn* passin' down;
> An' the old khansamah snorin'
>   On the bottle-khana floor,
> Like a Master in good standing
>   With my Mother-Lodge once more
>
> *Outside—'Sergeant! Sir! Salute! Salaam!'*
> *Inside—'Brother' an' it doesn't do no 'arm.*
> *We met upon the Level an' we parted on the Square,*
> *An' I was Junior Deacon in my Mother-Lodge out there!*

The English country is then no longer a place through which Britannia and Mr. Kipling can triumphantly tramp, but rather of continuity, memory, and present satisfaction. Under the trouble of an exile which is a greater burden than the official White Man's, the ends of the Empire remember the real English flowers. Against 'the old trail, our own trail, the out trail' lies 'the way through the woods'.

Other poems contain the same sense of equality and continuity. There is one which tells of a king building, and how the digging of foundations lays bare those of an earlier royalty, marked with the watchword: 'After me cometh a builder. Tell him I too have known'; and how, when the new building has to stop, the king caused the same sentence to be cut on all the abandoned works as a message to those who should follow him. There is a fascinating absurdity in which a blackhaired young man watches the building of flats near the Marble Arch, and the builders, amazed at all he knows of their craft, ask him his name.

> The young man kindly answered them:
> 'It might be Lot or Methusalem,
> Or it might be Moses (a man I hate),
> Whereas it is Pharaoh surnamed the Great.
>
> Your glazing is new and your plumbing's strange,
> But otherwise I perceive no change,
> And in less than a month, if you do as I bid,
> I'd learn you to build me a Pyramid.'

And this is followed by a similar 'strictly true' tale of 'Noah commanding the Ark'.

The poem on the Mother-Lodge contains this quatrain

> We 'adn't good regalia,
>   An' our Lodge was old an' bare,
> But we knew the Ancient Landmarks,
>   An' we kep' 'em to a hair;

and the last two lines suggest certain qualities in Mr. Kipling's imagination which have gone to shape his verse. The first is the 'Ancient Landmarks' themselves. This poet who has written on cruisers and aeroplanes and modern engines of all descriptions, who seems to be the very poet of machinery, is continually turning back to the beginnings of our race, and to those common things which unite the centuries. But one of those common things is the need, if the centuries are to be united at all, for a man to be efficient at his job, and to this need much of Mr. Kipling's verse recurs. Even the 'Upper Fourth Remove' are honoured, because it is they who are implicitly supposed to be exemplars, and along with these administrators are all the ordinary workers in all ages. The soldier, the sailor, the doctor, the poet, the peasant, all these, ancient and modern, are praised for the things they do and the true way they do them. The first of the ancient landmarks is the oldest rule in this book, that a man should do with his might what his hand findeth to do, whether it be with or against Fate, whether the result be good or bad, whether he be made more or less happy in the effort. Most poets have considered a little the desire for joy and peace that seems natural to man. But, though Mr. Kipling may at times allude to them, there is never the sense of joy or peace in his verse. Partly perhaps this is the fault of his rhythm and diction, both of which tend to be common, and by mere repetition to become commonplace. Partly it is due to an apparent lack of philosophical perspective; this poetry moves always in the foreground of the mind. His poems, intellectually speaking, are often two-dimensioned, and it is for this reason that the climax in some of them merely does not happen. This is so with nearly all the controversial verses—those on Ireland, on Pacificism, on the attitude of the Holy See during the War, on the cause of the Boer War, and so on. It is not that Mr. Kipling is necessarily wrong; it is that he gives us no idea of his opponents' having a case at all. His question in effect is always quite simply: 'My God, man, how can you be such a swine?' And, curiously enough, the 'My God' is not a mere oath; it is a quite sincere prayer—so much so that a more accurate implicit reading would be: 'My God, how can this man be such a swine?' Mr. Chesterton is occasionally casual enough in his controversies, but Mr. Kipling, in his annoyed disgust, merely abolishes the controversy. It creates exactly the same effect as that sentence which haunts more than one modern novelist—'He was the kind of man who called a napkin a serviette'; the unfortunate creature is left to 'the Wind that blows between the worlds' (which is presumably, though Mr. Kipling does not say so, the Wind of the Holy Ghost that blew on Pentecost), and we are left face to face with snobbishness.

But if Mr. Kipling has no use for the man who disagrees with him, he has certainly no more use for the inefficient man who agrees with him. He will forgive everything to the Upper Fourth Remove except slackness. In a short poem called *Mesopotamia: 1917*, he refused to pardon them as viciously as he refused in other poems to forgive Germans:

Shall we only threaten and be angry for an hour?
    When the storm is ended, shall we find
How softly but how swiftly they have sidled back to power
    By the favour and contrivance of their kind?

Even while they soothe us, while they promise large amends,
    Even while they make a show of fear,
Do they call upon their debtors, and take counsel with their friends,
    To confirm and re-establish each career?

If the rulers of England and Mr. Kipling's Empire were corrupt, if justice were sold or the seats of justice defiled, and he knew it, it is certain that his voice would be the loudest in protest. It is very likely that he would not know it; but there is a poem called *Gehazi*, dated 1915, apparently on some appointment to the Justiciary, which has something of this anger—

    Well done, well done, Gehazi!
      Stretch forth thy ready hand,
    Thou barely 'scaped from judgement,
      Take oath to judge the land
    Unswayed by gift of money
      Or privy bribe, more base,
    Of knowledge which is profit
      In any market-place . . .
      Stand up, stand up, Gehazi!
        Draw close thy robe and go,
    Gehazi, Judge in Israel,
      A leper white as snow.

But the difficulty with this poem and with others

is their topicality. They are, in that sense, journalistic. Dates are already needed for many of them, and are already useless for many. 'We forget so soon', as another doctrinal poet has said; and if there is no greatness of style to help us keep the poems, and therefore their occasions, in memory, what is to become of Mr. Kipling's reputation?

The answer is in the second of those ancient landmarks, and this time it is an outstanding one. It is, quite simply, death. But this landmark is set up, not so much in the poems that call attention to it—the *Hymn before Action*, for example—as in the narratives. And the narratives are some of Mr. Kipling's best work.

For one thing, the efficiency which he has praised befriends him; for another, he has no opponents; for another, his metres are as straightforward as, and therefore of use to, his stories; for another, his choice of words is equally simple and direct; for another, the very 'imperialism' which may, for some readers, destroy the effectiveness of his hortatory or comminatory poems, is here of use. When he says, in effect, of England that she 'hath taken toll of the North and South—[her] glory reacheth far,' our minds are on guard immediately, but no one minds it being said of 'Abdur Rahman, the Durani chief'. There may be doctrine hidden in the roll of the English cities; there is no after-thought for us in

> The herald read his titles forth;
>   We set the logs aglow:
> 'Friend of the English, free from fear,
> Baron of Luni to Jeysulmeer,
> Lord of the desert of Bikaneer,
>   King of the Jungle, go!'

These advantages make admirable things of the tales—*The Ballad of the King's Mercy*, *The Ballad of the King's Jest*, *With Scindia to Delhi*, *The Ballad of East and West*, *Shiv and the Grasshopper*, *Tomlinson*, and the rest. But most of them, and nearly all of the best, are sharpened to a point of death or the nearness of death. In that point it is only honour or the lack of honour that is felt, whenever there is anything beyond the mere story to be felt at all. And this honour is also, in a sense, efficiency. As a man's ability for his job should be clean and sure, so should his soul be able to meet the extreme of Fate unterrified, and it is Fate that he has to meet—Fate and no other kind of god, though in some of his lesser poems Mr. Kipling gives it divine names, 'Jehovah of the Thunders' and so on. There are even one or two poems in which the persons of the Christian myth are introduced: the Child Jesus, and an occasional Madonna. But they are not very convincing. The real force which appears, aboriginal and almost irresistible, is not the energy of those mortal and deific figures. Another religion has captured Mr. Kipling; he is the nearest to a Mahommedan poet that the English have produced. It is not only the poems in which he borrows the phraseology of Islam that make one say so; the name Allah in *The Answer* or in *The Legend of Mirth*, or (from the last) such lines as

> the shining Courts were void
> Save for one Seraph whom no charge employed,
> With folden wings and slumber-threatened brow,
> To whom The Word: 'Beloved, what dost thou?'
> 'By the Permission', came the answer soft,
> 'Little I do nor do that little oft.

As is The Will in Heaven so on earth
Where by The Will I strive to make men mirth.'

More strongly this Force is felt in the tempest at sea and the famine on land, the desert and the pestilence, the natural forces against which his chosen heroes conduct their successful or unsuccessful war, and combined with these the mere law of cause and effect which he proclaims so often, the fact that inefficiency produces disaster. No excuse however good, no reason however weighty, can turn aside the Law, and Mr. Kipling is passionately in love with that Law. Even more than he dislikes his intellectual opponents he despises those who try to avoid it or are surprised at the results of its existence.

> We had a kettle; we let it leak:
>   Our not repairing it made it worse.
> We haven't had any tea for a week...
>   The bottom is out of the Universe!

It may be because of this that his sea poems are so good, because the sea is the best image of that element in life which cannot be persuaded or overcome, but with which every fight must be a drawn battle; and because of this that his high figures are great in death, because death comes to all and the Law wins in the end. So his Queen Elizabeth, haunted by ghosts, meets them boldly.

The Queen was in her chamber, her sins were on her head.
She looked the spirits up and down and statelily she said:—
'Backward and forward and sideways though I've been,
Yet I am Harry's daughter and I am England's Queen.'

But the Law is found in yet another place, in machinery. In *M'Andrew's Hymn* a Scotch engineer compares the working of the engines of the ship to Calvinism, and indeed Calvinism, like Islam, found the secret of the universe in the unchanging Will. So in many poems, and by many ways, we come back to the same central idea. Nor is it the idea only that relates machinery to Mr. Kipling's verse. To say it is machine-made would be silly. But so many of the poems do seem to jingle—now and then deliberately, as in the light verse on the 'jingling tonga-bar', but generally because obviously he thinks and feels in that way. It is machinery—these rhythms and rhymes—but it is conscious machinery. They are machine-emotions, machine-thoughts (or, in another simile, herd-emotions and herd-thoughts). But they know that they are so, and have so chosen to be—their nature being also their choice—and therefore they are in the end saved from the dreadful curse of nonentity. They are machinery, but they are. The rattle and clang are tiring sometimes and sometimes irritating, but they are not negligible. It has been said that nearly all Mr. Kipling's verse would be poetry, if only a poet had written it; it would be truer to say that most of his verse is not poetry though a poet has written it. But if it persuades us that he is a poet, whereas the verse of other more solemn and humane and high-principled writers does not, it has at least achieved a not insignificant result.

The best-known part of his work is the poems of life in the army; the *Barrack Room Ballads* and their like. But if they are important, it is not because they show us the modern soldier, or tell us of his hardships or heroism—that might make them valuable for sociology or ethics, but not for poetry. It is because with them a new and peculiar sound entered English verse. Universal emotions were expressed in a new technique. Taken as a whole, it might be doubted whether any poems, for all their Cockney slang, were less like the English soldier. They may express him or not; none but he (and of course there is no such being) could possibly say. But they have a high, feverish, bitter, unhappy note, which is quite unparalleled. This fever and unhappiness are not the speculations of the study; they arise from mists endured and wounds suffered and vigils kept. 'The Widow at Windsor' has been one of Mr. Kipling's most popular phrases. But each stanza of the semi-patriotic poem so called is sprinkled with an ironical bitterness in parentheses.

> (Poor beggars! it's blue with our bones!) . . .
>
> (Poor beggars! it's always they guns!) . . .
>
> Take 'old o' the Wings o' the Mornin',
>   An' flop round the earth till you're dead;
> But you won't get away from the tune that they play
>   To the bloomin' old rag over 'ead.
>   (Poor beggars!—it's 'ot over 'ead!) . . .
>
>   (Poor beggars!—they'll never see 'ome!)

It is impossible to prove this by quotation; single lines could not do it, for the agony runs through the realism and the patriotism and the humour. There are, of course, poems without it (such as *The Shut-eye Sentry*); there are poems in which it is almost the only thing, such as *Ford o' Kabul River*, *That Day*, *Cholera Camp*, *The Sergeant's Wedding*, and '*Snarleyow*'. There have been many easier and cheaper patriots than Mr. Kipling, but few who have been so conscious of the daily price paid by the servants of patriotism. He had commented, long before Mr. Sassoon, on the ways of an inefficient High Command—

> The General 'ad ' produced a great effect',
>   The General 'ad the country cleared—almost,
> The General ' 'ad no reason to expect',
>   And the Boers 'ad us bloomin' well on toast . . .
>   An' it all went into the laundry,
>   But it never came out in the wash . . .

He had put into a poem on marching something of the intense horror it describes—

Try—try—try—try—to think o' something different—
O—my—God—keep—me from goin' lunatic!
(Boots—boots—boots—boots—movin' up an' down again!)
  There's no discharge in the war!

Count—count—count—count—the bullets in the bandoliers.
If—your—eyes—drop—they will get atop o' you
(Boots—boots—boots—boots—movin' up an' down again!)—
  There's no discharge in the war!

Here and there, on the edge of this particular universe, something of a terrifying threat hovers. The youth who hung in the branches of a tree over the bayonets of the King's guard in the *Ballad of the King's Jest*; the malicious laughter in the *Sergeant's Wedding*:

> Cheer for the Sergeant's weddin'—
>   Give 'em one cheer more!
> Grey gun-'orses in the lando,
>   And a rogue is married to, &c.,

the 'Baa! Baa! Baa!' in *Gentlemen-Rankers*—these

and other things are a reminder that this poetry is not confined to the superficial emotions of club or pub. *The Passing of Danny Deever* might rank with Wilde's *Ballad of Reading Gaol*. In these moments there is vocalized, sometimes in a thin shriek, sometimes in a note of deeper endurance, the loneliness of the soul. And the answer comes in the poems of a passionate brotherhood. Wars and controversies and the tumults of a day have caused Mr. Kipling to shrill out his curses against the enemies of a day; the cloud that ascends from them has perhaps blinded his sight and certainly hidden from us his high concern. The Upper Fourth Remove, the barrack-room Cockneys, are followers of chivalry and Romance. In two poems Mr. Kipling has spoken of that Romance. The first is called *The King*, and describes how every age sees Romance in a by-gone period and not in its own, as ours does. But

> His hand was on the lever laid,
>   His oil-can soothed the worrying cranks,
> His whistle waked the snowbound grade,
>   His fog-horn cut the reeking Banks;
> By dock and deep and mine and mill
> The Boy-god reckless laboured still.

This is the lesser romance, efficiency and order and achievement. But there is another, since every god known to man has a greater deity in its nature of which we only dream; and this is the *True Romance*.

> Thy face is far from this our war,
>   Our call and counter-cry;
> I shall not find Thee quick and kind,
>   Nor know Thee till I die.

> Enough for me in dreams to see
>   And touch Thy garments' hem:
> Thy feet have trod so near to God
>   I may not follow them.

This is the Romance to which man looks for salvation 'in the hour of death and in the day of judgement', the spirit of an inner virginity which should accompany and produce the outer efficiency. It is in the ritual where the praise of both is mingled that Mr. Kipling has sung his part. In the Mother-Lodge set up in the desolation of the world, not only does the remembrance of other things 'do no harm', but it is the one necessity, and the writer of the smallest versicles, in whatever language, is fortunate. Mr. Kipling has described his own office.

> Outside—'Sergeant! Sir! Salute! Salaam!'
> Inside—'Brother', and it doesn't do no 'arm.
> We met upon the Level an' we parted on the Square,
> An' I was Junior Deacon in my Mother-Lodge out there!

End Piece

End Piece

Caesar stood on the ramparts
   of the farthest Roman wall,
with the camps and marches behind him
   that meant a conquered Gaul;
and wide before him a ghostly sea:
saying: 'And what may Britain be?'

Caesar stood on the ramparts,
   hearing how boatmen hear
the calling ghosts at midnight
   and rise in haste and fear
those travellers o'er the straits to row;
saying: 'Where the ghosts go Rome may go.'

Caesar stood on the ramparts
   having found, on many a field,
how Fate may turn a finger
   and break the stoutest shield;
but holding a steadfast mind within
saying: 'What of the recruits' discipline?'

Caesar stood on the ramparts,
   and looked o'er the curving foam,
with the stout centurions by him,
   and the eagles and ranks of Rome:
saying: 'Bid the ships do thus and thus,'
making a province, a world, and us.

WILLIAM BUTLER YEATS

Born in Dublin, 1865. He studied art for a while, but afterwards devoted himself to literature, gaining a European reputation of sufficient strength to bring him the Nobel prize in 1923—the year after he had become a Senator of the Irish Free State. He has been among the chief figures of the Irish literary movement, and a manager of the Abbey Theatre, Dublin. His poems include: *The Wanderings of Oisin*, 1889; *The Countess Cathleen*, 1892; *Poems*, 1895; *The Secret Rose*, 1897; *The Wind among the Reeds*, 1899; *The Shadowy Waters*, 1900; *Cathleen ni Hoolihan*, 1902; *Hour Glass and Other Plays*, 1904; *The King's Threshold*, 1904; *Deidre*, 1907; collected edition, 8 vols., 1908; *The Green Helmet and other Poems*, 1910; *Plays for an Irish Theatre*, 1912; *The Wild Swans of Coole*, 1919; *Seven Poems and a Fragment*, 1922; *The Tower*, 1928.

No one who, in the days of youth, and with no particular knowledge of the author, has opened the volume of Mr. Yeats's poems which contains *The Countess Cathleen*, and has recognized after the first half-dozen lines that he was reading a poet of quite peculiar poignancy—a poet of all but the very greatest importance; and who has, later, seen Mr. Yeats at the old Coronet Theatre in Notting Hill, and joined in the tumultuous shouts that greeted him— no one who has had these experiences can feel, when he begins to write of him, quite as if he were writing about any ordinary poet. And this feeling is accentuated when he finds that, twenty years afterwards, and through all the intervening period, while other poets have risen and faded, and expectations have been aroused and disappointed, the conviction that this is one of the poets has remained unshaken; that the same voice is uttering changed but still beautiful and enduring poetry to changed ears; and that one who is still living is already of classic importance.

The thing is so obvious that the pleasure of the personal recollection must be invoked to excuse it. About the right of Mr. Hardy, Mr. Chesterton, Mr. Kipling, even (surprisingly) Mr. Bridges, to the title, there have been occasional disputes; no one has ever challenged that of Mr. Yeats, or rather of the first Mr. Yeats. Of the second Mr. Yeats, of him who began to write somewhere between 1904 and 1912, there has been a good deal more discussion. People who had grown to regard him as (in the lowest sense) 'poetic', and who, it seems likely, regarded all poetry as being a kind of rich decoration of life, objected to this poetry becoming at times almost violent and certainly insolent. Mr. Yeats's business, it seems to have been felt, was to go on longing for Innisfree and nine bean-rows, and not to be sometimes rude to, and sometimes positively contemptuous of, his fellows. Where were the 'dreams'? Where were the Rose and the august hierarchies and those

> Who rise, wing above wing, flame above flame,
> And, like a storm, cry the Ineffable Name?

Besides, he was so efficient at it. A few of his quatrains are the quintessence of insult; as for example that

On hearing the Students of our New University have joined the Agitation against Immoral Literature

> Where, where but here have Pride and Truth
> That long to give themselves for wage
> To shake their wicked sides at youth
> Restraining reckless middle-age?

Or that other poem to a wealthy man 'who promised a second subscription to the Dublin Municipal Gallery if it were proved that people wanted pictures'; where Duke Ercole and Guidobaldi and Cosimo de Medici are shown, in a scathing comparison, spending themselves on art without asking whether the onion-sellers wanted it, or what was the shepherds' will.

Is this the voice of the dreamer, the faery student, the occultist, the lover of beauty? Well, it might very well (*mutatis mutandis*) be the voice of Landor or of Donne, and it is with those two poets that Mr. Yeats has spoken of dining at his journey's end. Neither of those was satisfied with mere wandering and sighing over beauty; there was in each of them a restless mind, an insolent heart, a high and inquiring soul. And if we can believe Mr. Yeats's claim, we must attribute to him something of the same great qualities. They are perhaps most obvious in his prose —especially in that learned and profound work which is called *A Vision: An Explanation of Life, founded upon the writings of Giraldus and upon certain doctrines attributed to Kusta ben Laka*—but they are obvious enough in his verse, except to those who are satisfied with the anthological repetition of *Innisfree*, of which Mr. Yeats must be as tired as Alice Meynell was of the *Letter from a Girl to her own Old Age*. They are obvious, for example, in some of the love-poems, which recall no later manner than that of the seventeenth century metaphysicals, in their insolence and passion and wit—which is something more than our modern wit. The poem which ends 'Tread softly because you tread on my dreams' (and a very beautiful poem it is) is almost as popular as *Innisfree*; not so that other which ends:

> They have spoken against you everywhere,
> But weigh this song with the great and their pride;
> I made it out of a mouthful of air,
> Their children's children shall say they have lied.

Nor that description of

> A woman, of so shining loveliness,
> That men threshed corn at midnight by a tress,
> A little stolen tress.

Nor that other which speaks of a

>   mind
> That nobleness made simple as a fire,
> With beauty like a tightened bow, a kind
> That is not natural in an age like this,
> Being high and solitary and most stern?
> Why, what could she have done being what she is?
> Was there another Troy for her to burn?

'Was there another Troy for her to burn?' We have lost that particular great style since the Elizabethans and their immediate successors, except in Mr. Yeats's verse. But the kinship between his voice and theirs is not only in the lyrics but, for example, in *The Countess Cathleen*, where, on the third page, the phrase 'gilding your tongue with the calamitous times' might have come from some Elizabethan, as might the other, 'Leave lonely the long-hoarding surges'. The differences are obvious enough, but the likeness is there too, the young Marlowe as well as Donne seems to be recalled by this poet whose 'aspiring mind' is also concerned with 'the wondrous architecture of the world'. Nor is it only in their magniloquence that he is like them, but in their worldliness; his feet are planted as firmly on the earth as theirs are. For all its merchants from hell, its vision of warring angels, its wandering musician and lonely castle in the woods, *The Countess Cathleen* opens with a phrase as common as Shakespeare's 'night's candles'—'You are all thumbs'. The scene between the demon-merchants and the peasant-folk is very nearly dramatic, and only not quite so because it seems to be gathered up and made part of that piercing music which masters all Mr. Yeats's poetry. It is perhaps for the same reason that the humorous scenes in *The King's Threshold* jar a little; our ears are too attuned to a sound such as no other poet has given us to consent to be deafened, even for a minute or two, by what so many other writers can do so well. The challenging stupidity of the earth, the dull cruelty and uncomeliness of it, these we can endure, for these do but throw up the high and angry opposition that is here. But mere fun—no. It is a limitation, perhaps, a necessary condition of this intense strain of music, but how willingly we assent to it!

But there is a more important difference—or more important anyhow for our purpose—between Mr. Yeats and the Elizabethans, and it is in the countries they have separately explored. A still half-fabulous world provided the earlier poets with inventions, myths, and dreams. But for us all strangeness, most adventure, and in a growing sense all space, must be found within. It is rather in ideas of the world than in the world that novelty and familiarity must lie, and it is by the recognition of the inner in the outer that most of us find satisfaction, by the accommodation of the phenomenal world to our beliefs and consistencies. How far that world is patient of our imposed interpretations—whether they be those of ancient or modern science—is another matter, and one fortunately which need not be discussed in speaking of poetry. For we are then primarily concerned not with how just any poet's myth of the universe may be, how far we may expect to be able to make our own actualities correspond with it, but only with how he sees and states it. Elements or elementals, both are credible then (and for that matter at any other time also).

Mr. Yeats, exploring the nature of the world, has come down heavily on the side of the elementals, and of all else that may be implied by a theory of the universe which has a place for such beings. He speaks of them as simply as of 'Davis, Mangann, Ferguson', and in the same poem.

> Know, that I would accounted be
> True brother of that company,
> Who sang to sweeten Ireland's wrong,
> Ballad and story, rann and song . . .
> Nor may I less be counted one
> With Davis, Mangan, Ferguson,
> Because to him who ponders well
> My rhymes more than their rhyming tell
> Of the dim wisdoms old and deep
> That God gives unto man in sleep.
> For the elemental beings go
> About my table to and fro . . .

No couplet in literature has more emotional sense of what it says, or causes us more easily to accept it.

The incantation seems to work without and not merely within; it is a poem, but it is also a charm—it seems magical not only as invocation of the Muse but as evocation of other powers. It is not without regret that one realizes that magic is not so easily communicated to the casual reader. But magic and the possibilities of magic are continually present to the thought of Mr. Yeats's verse, whether as subject or as allusion. In *The Countess Cathleen* the demons call to 'the elemental populace' to carry away the gold they have stolen; in *Lines Written in Dejection* he laments that

> All the wild witches those most noble ladies
> For all their broomsticks and their tears,
> Their angry tears, are gone.

(And again we may remember the Elizabethan 'Her angry eyes are great with tears'—so easily is association set up.) In *Ego Dominus Tuus* he makes one of the dramatic characters speak of tracing

> Enthralled by the unconquerable delusion,
> Magical shapes:

though it is noteworthy that this poem goes on to become a serious piece of literary criticism and discussion of the nature of creative art.

Besides magic there is faery. More in the earlier poems than in the later, Mr. Yeats concerned himself, at times, with that world which is said to exist invisibly in this one,

> Where beauty has no ebb, decay no flood,
> But joy is wisdom, Time an endless song.

In *The Land of Heart's Desire*, from which those lines come, a mortal girl is lured away by a faery visitor; in *The Stolen Child* the faery song accompanies a child to that happier state 'from a world more full of weeping than he can understand'; in *A Faery Song*, 'sung by the people of faery over Diarmuid and Grania', the lovers are promised 'rest far from men'.

But magic and faery, and those other old alchemical wisdoms in which Mr. Yeats has found interest, what is their poetic value? It is perhaps the continual suggestion of other possibilities than the normal mind is conscious of. Since this verse does not give us (as naturally it could not) instruction how to work spells and practise the true alchemy and discover faerie kingdoms, we are not concerned with it as practical doctrine; it is but the effect of these continual apostrophes, invocations, and visions, to which we look. And so looking we must not omit one other vision which haunts this longing and desirous verse —the vision of a final attainment more perfect than faerie, the dream of the Rose, the Red Rose of beatitude and peace. In the poem previously quoted in which Mr. Yeats speaks of the singers of Ireland and of the elemental beings, he says also that

> The red-rose-bordered hem
> Of her whose history began
> Before God made the angelic clan
> Trails all about the written page...
> And still the thoughts of Ireland brood
> Upon her holy quietude,

nor are this poet's thoughts the least quick to brood on that consolation.

Nowhere perhaps is the whole purport of this desire set out more exactly than in the talk between

Forgael and Aibric in *The Shadowy Waters*. On the deck of a ship sailing on extreme waters towards the end of the world, among mutinous sailors, the master Forgael disputes with his only faithful follower Aibric on the nature of experience. Aibric is willing to take the world and all the pleasures of the world for what they are worth, attributing the discontent that follows them to the dreams of youth, and losing that melancholy in other similar pleasures. But Forgael is in search of something else—

> Miracle, ecstasy, the impossible hope,
> The flagstone under all, the fire of fires,
> The roots of the world.

That which is dream to the other is to him the promise of the real and intense life, of which this is but the image on the mirror.

> What the world's million lips are searching for
> Must be substantial somewhere.

Especially in love is this contradiction of the world's proof to be found. Aibric says that 'all that ever loved have loved' in the common way', 'brief longing and deceiving hope and bodily tenderness'; in spite of the disappointment that ensues 'there is no other way'. But Forgael answers him in piercing and prophetic lines—

> Yet never have two lovers kissed but they
> Believed there was some other near at hand
> And almost wept because they could not find it.

In the world of dreams 'that to the sense Is shadow' is

> the flowing, changing world
> That the heart longs for.

'Dreams' is a word that occurs often enough in Mr. Yeats's work, but it seems that we should do him wrong if we took it to mean only the confused nonsense of our own sleep. It may include that, but it is more than that; it is more than the refuge of the minor poet and weak artist who so often claim for their negligible fantasies the attention of the world which has, if nothing better, at least something as good to concern itself with. It is more even than the beautiful vaguenesses which Mr. Yeats himself has sometimes made for us out of his own lesser imaginations. It is prophecy, it is vision, it is sight of and belief in a mode of existence much more real and intense than that of every day. It is the hunger for that mode of being which, in the earlier poems with lament, in the later with a certain bitterness, causes Mr. Yeats to think of the world of 'bankers, schoolmasters, and clergymen'. The poetry itself is proof enough of his sincerity; no such beauty, no such vivid insolence, ever sprang from a mind that was not set with all its strength of desire upon some other than a mortal end. But what was once, so beautiful was the verse, in the earlier poems a sorrow to linger in, an exquisite sadness in the heart of love, has become in the later a real suffering. 'Time and Fate and Change' were spoken of dramatically, or else woven into the tapestries of the chamber of love; but in later days they themselves help to make the verse.

>A pity beyond all telling
>Is hid in the heart of love—

but the poignancy of it was, even so, a sweet enjoyment. Sorrow will not consent even so tenderly to be lulled with words, and Mr. Yeats would be a lesser poet than he is if grief and disaster did not also speak in his verse. There are no more beautiful poems in English than some of his laments for 'dear dead women'—

> A crowd
> Will gather and not know it walks the very street
> Whereon a thing once walked that seemed a burning cloud;

and that exquisite one which has for refrain

> I knew a phoenix in my youth, so let them have their day.

Over the political poems, too, a change has come. 'Romantic Ireland's dead and gone', but the poem that says so is itself a contradiction. The anger which an aristocratic and poetic mind feels for the corruption and greed and malice of his fellows, and for the blatant stupidities of the crowd, his scorn and his despair, are at least equalled by the poems on the heroes of the Easter Rebellion—'a terrible beauty is born'—in one of which he deliberately includes among that great company one who had done his own dear friends 'most bitter wrong':

> He too has been changed in his turn,
> Transformed utterly,
> A terrible beauty is born.

In another poem, *The People*, where he laments—almost fretfully—that all he has tried to do for the town has been wasted, and that he might have been living all that time, in ease and according to his desire, in Italy, he puts also into the mouth of 'his phoenix' the grave reply that, though 'the drunkards, pilferers of public funds', have done her grievous harm,

> 'Yet never have I, now nor any time,
> Complained of the people.'
>   All I could reply
> Was: 'You, that have not lived in thought but deed,
> Can have the purity of a natural force,
> But I, whose virtues are the definitions
> Of the analytic mind, can neither close
> The eye of the mind, nor keep my tongue from speech.'
> And yet, because my heart leaped at her words,
> I was abashed, and now they come to mind
> After nine years, I sink my head abashed.

This mind, that was set, like Donne's, on other modes of being, has engaged itself also with the world, and out of that conflict has made (as it was its business to do) most moving verse. 'Out of the strong came forth sweetness'. The marvellous song of these earlier years, the inappeasable desire which was sometimes a lament, and sometimes a tenderness, and sometimes an incantation, and sometimes a questing call after faerie, and sometimes a cry so near the borders of humanity that only the songs of Ariel went beyond it—all these things have changed and yet still exist.

The change is clear, not only in the tone of the mind, but in the sound of the verse. If there was a danger to the earlier poems it was that the slight languor which seemed sometimes to accompany those dreams should be changed into a slight weariness with them, through the over-repetition of certain words and phrases—'pearl-pale', 'dim hair', 'white feet', and so on. In its weaker moments (since all poetry must have its weaker moments) the

verse sank a little towards a blurred emotionalism.
Compare, for example, the too rhetorical note of

> My master will break up the sun and moon,
> And quench the stars in the ancestral night
> And overturn the thrones of God and the angels,

with the much better rhetoric of

> You shall hang
> Nailed like dead vermin to the doors of God,

and with the restrained poetry of

> We must be tender with all budding things.
> Our Maker let no thought of Calvary
> Trouble the morning stars in their first song.

If anything troubled us when we heard Mr. Yeats's first song it was an anxiety whether this music, ghostly in all senses of the word, could go on. It has reassured us by taking a new movement, under which the older is still felt, sometimes in opposition, sometimes in alliance. Lines such as

> We that are old, old and gay,
> O so old,
> Thousands of years, thousands of years,
> If all were told,

have tended to speak more like those other lines on Dante, 'the chief imagination of Christendom',

> He found the unpersuadable justice, he found
> The most exalted lady loved by a man.

There is still something of a sigh in that last line, but it is the inevitable sigh of humanity.

There is another thing, besides awakening our minds to dreams, more or less imaged in actuality, which Mr. Yeats has done. He has given to English verse, and made native to it, a new mythology. Until he wrote, our literature had had, on the whole, three mythologies to draw on—the Greek and the Norse and the Christian; now it has also the Celtic. Names and shapes unapprehended till now are now its possession; its boundaries are so far enlarged. This certainly is an accident of time and place and genius, but it is an accident for which we can hardly be too grateful. It is less of an accident that he has renewed in us the sense of great interior possibilities by his use of the traditions of magic and faerie, and made his own verse tremble with their imagined presence. It is by the most happy accident of his personal genius that he has given to us so large a number of poems of beauty and power, so many memorable lines, that we may say to him, in his own phrase,

> our bodies have begun to dream,
> And you have grown to be a burning sod
> In the imagination and intellect.

End Piece

The ecstasy of adoration dies;
    speaking with four strong poets other than you,
    I have felt the frenzy half itself renew,
worshipping, trembling, a fool where they were wise:
but O the crowded theatre, and the cries
    shaking the dark air, if so loud a cue
    might bid you speak! the tumult still runs through
my memory and my dreams, and still my eyes
behold you solitary, when the show
    was done, sweet music making an end thereof,
    shutting the sorrow and pageant of Cathleen:
was it a marvel I adored you so,
    being twenty, a poetaster, never in love,
    and you the only poet I had seen?

WILLIAM HENRY DAVIES

Born 1871. *The Autobiography of a Super-Tramp* (1908) and *Later Days* (1925) contain his autobiography, including his experiences as a tramp and pedlar in America and England, and as a cattleman on voyages between those countries, his mode of publication of his first book and its success. This book was *The Soul's Destroyer* (1906); among those which have followed it have been *New Poems* (1907), *Nature Poems* (1908), *Farewell to Poesy* (1910), *Songs of Joy* (1911), and other smaller books, two series of *Collected Poems* (1916 and 1923), and a complete collection in 1928.

IF, as Mr. Davies tells us, he hears men say

'This Davies has no depth,
He writes of birds, of staring cows and sheep,
And throws no light on deep, eternal things,'

he might ask them what kind of depth they want. Into what particular mysteries do these critics demand that a poet's abysses shall open?

It is true, of course, that Mr. Davies's work is nearly all lyric, and most of it very short lyric at that. It is true that a short lyric cannot climb down and up and about the peaks and pits of being as can a *Macbeth* or a *Prelude* or a *Ring and the Book*. But it may, in a dozen lines, throw itself from one edge of such a pit to the other, so that the reader catches a sense of profundity; or it may sit on a peak or tall tree, singing so high and sweet and distant that the reader longs to discover such possibilities in his own mind. It seems a little unfair to insist that such sudden emotional shocks ought to be accompanied also by slow exploration. And the fact (if it is a fact) that we have grown a little used to Mr. Davies is a criticism of our capacity, not of his. So also is the undoubted fact that his reputation is only that of a simple pastoral poet, who writes of 'staring cows and sheep'. So, finally, is the reported accusation that, even in those poems, he 'has no depth'.

Three failures to contemplate a poet's mind rightly is a serious matter; are we indeed so careless? and if we are, is there any excuse?

With the exception of Mr. Housman's, most of Mr. Davies's poems are probably shorter than those of any other modern writer. Of the *Collected Poems* two hundred and seventy are of three stanzas or less, or of a roughly equivalent length. It is therefore obvious that Mr. Davies normally has to get his effect at once or not at all. He has to be immediately memorable; neither he nor the reader has time to turn round. It has been said of other poets who wrote such short verse that they carved heads on cherry-stones; the obvious contrast between the cherry-stone and the cherry will serve to distinguish their work from that of Mr. Davies. For our admiration, our wonder, at his is not an admiration of dexterity and craftsmanship, however high and delicate, but of a ripe growth, a richness that springs from some world of experience common to him and us; even though we have never chanced to meet a rainbow and a cuckoo together—

> A rainbow and a cuckoo, Lord,
>   How rich and great the times are now;

or to have noticed the mark of birds' feet—

> But what gives me most joy is when I see
>   Snow on my doorstep, printed by their feet.

The delicate, beautiful, and immortal detail would serve as a simile for Mr. Davies's poems; they alight and take flight again, and leave us looking at the entrance to our minds—'snow on my doorstep, printed by their feet'.

One after another of these poems leaves some such detail with us; a unique moment suddenly exists. It may be an interior or an exterior experience

> My heart has many a sweet bird's song—
> And one that's all my own.
>
> . . . . .
>
> Look you, how he stands and sings,
> Half-way up his legs in snow.
>
> . . . . .
>
> That toad's dark life must be my own,
> Buried alive inside a stone.

And so on. It would be easier to quote whole poems than lines, for of these poems by far the greater number are each of them a complete unity, and the moment of appreciation is in and through the whole. It is the instantaneous response to the instantaneous appeal of the instant.

But it is not only with the hitherto unnoticed detail that Mr. Davies takes the reader by storm; it is also by his intensity. There is a diffused feeling that his chief business is to 'stand and stare', and it may be freely admitted that the word 'stare' occurs with a frequency that is all but amusing.

> What is this life if, full of care,
> We have no time to stand and stare?

> cows that keep
> On staring that I stand so long.

> The moon was dying with a stare.
> I must become a starer too
>
> Who dreams a sweeter life than this,
> To stand and stare . . .

so the word, and (in other words) the idea, reiterates itself. But it may be a deceptive word, for it implies a condition as intense as, though otherwise very different from, that of Wordsworth when he demanded a wise passiveness. Both these poets have in them a wild and violent life; it is only the careless reader who supposes that they are indolently contented. It is true that Mr. Davies is chiefly concerned with the effect that Nature produces on his eyes, while Wordsworth was concerned with what Nature did to and for his philosophy. There is no mysticism, true or false, in the later poet; although he occasionally drops into something remarkably like the pathetic fallacy. For instance *The Example* begins

> Here's an example from
> A Butterfly;
> That on a rough, hard rock
> Happy can lie;

and goes on to encourage the poet to make his joy

> like this
> Small Butterfly.

The Butterfly may, of course, be happy; no one can tell. The probability would seem rather against it, and in favour of supposing that it knew something was wrong, without knowing what. But that also would be to attribute man's consciousness to the insect; agnosticism is a wiser mood.

This attribution, however, is a rare thing in Mr. Davies; he would probably have gained a greater reputation for 'depth' if there had been more of it. His 'staring' on the whole receives the object clearly and fairly; and that is because of the fineness of the matter he opposes to it—his eye, his mind, and his genius. Their nature has been defined in a number of poems; two may be used as examples. In one he begins, 'Come, thou sweet Wonder'; in another, walking on the Embankment before five in the morning, he sees first of all the outcasts and then the early workers. Of the first

> These people have no work, thought I,
> And long before their time they die;

of the second

> These people work too hard, thought I,
> And long before their time they die.

Between these two kinds of men the poet seems to walk as if they were already dead, and he only were living in the true world, a world of vivid amazement and intense joy, a world of sunrises and cows and sheep and owls and cuckoos and toads and butterflies and squirrels and pears and the grass and snow printed with birds' feet.

> The horses, kine, and sheep did seem
> As they would vanish for a dream;

they seem so, but they are definitely not a dream. It is 'Early Morn'; there is nothing of the supernatural or fantastic about these precise objects precisely rendered—only a never-ending amazement at them. Mr. Davies has shown us man being what Mr. Chesterton has told us he ought to be—surprised.

And he has, it must be admitted, given us more to be surprised at; he has communicated his wonder rather than indoctrinated us with the gospel. The very nature of his verse does it; as he with the sheep, so we with his poems can only stand and stare. It is so astonishing that a poem could be just like that. It is astonishing that birds' feet should mark the snow; but it is also astonishing that we can know it and delight in it. After all, why should we be so pleased? It is that absurdity that dances, unseen but present, through so much of Mr. Davies's verse.

This, however, does not help us with the dreadful accusation of 'want of depth'; what is to be done about that? The simplest thing is to read through, at as near one sitting as possible, either of the series of *Collected Poems*. They cannot, of course, be appreciated as poems so: one a day, or at most two, with the day between them, is a safer way of ensuring that. But as they follow one another through the reader's mind they create a sensation of remarkable variety. The majority are 'nature poems' certainly, but what a number of other subjects there are! Infancy, children, the poet's friends and acquaintances, death, sickness, poetry, money, eating and drinking, sleep, age, the outcast poor, sailors, music, a blind child, the lodging-house fire, religion; and besides all these two particular groups of poems—the love poems and those on the moods of the mind. It seems, with such a list before us, difficult to think of a subject Mr. Davies has not found for his verse. It is clear anyhow that his 'staring' has been universal; he no more, again, than Wordsworth has neglected the human heart by which we live.

Nor is it at all possible to say that he has merely gone on expressing an indefatigable surprise. The stare has become a more conscious watchfulness; the poems may be as short, but they come to us as the Jacobean lyrics do after the Elizabethan—with an effect of a considerate, if not always subtle, intellect. The facts are still simple, but there are more than one of them in each poem, they are not infrequently opposed, and they open to the mind a complexity of universal experience. The language is still simple, and very occasionally it happens that this simplicity is almost overdone. *Nell Barnes* hovers on the edge of failure, although it saves itself at the last. It is an account, in five stanzas, of how

> They lived apart for three long years,
> Bill Barnes and Nell his wife,

each making up for the separation in other ways. But when Nell passed the shop, saw it empty, and heard that her husband had gone 'five thousand miles away',

> She sickened from that day.

> To see his face was health and life,
> And when it was denied,
> She could not eat, and broke her heart,—
> It was for love she died.

The contradiction is at once credible and profound, but the simplicity that so expresses it is the simplicity of a catholic feeling for the passion of man. This is shown no less in another poem called *The Idiot and the Child*.

> There was a house where an old dame
> Lived with a son, his child and wife;
> And with a son of fifty years,
> An idiot all his life.

The child 'who loved her life so well' dies.
>This made the idiot chuckle hard:
>The old dame looked at that child dead
>And him she loved—'Ah, well; thank God
>It is no worse!' she said.

Some of these poems have in them an implicit criticism of social life, like that 'lesson for fathers' (*The Little Ones*) which tells how two children, expecting presents at Christmas, found none (because their parents had come home drunk), and supposed that they themselves had 'done some wrong'. It is dreadful to think of such an imposition on a child's mind, of a teaching which makes a child believe that he himself has caused what is actually the mere malevolence of things or others' faults.

It may be this habit of observation and this knowledge of intensity that have helped to cause those heavy moods in Mr. Davies of which in some poems he speaks, so far as those moods can be attributable to any cause, 'the heavy rain of care' and the dark hour 'which is not born of care'. The sadness common to us all lies under a number of these swift lyrics; they soar up from it, but, agile and lovely as they are, they do not forget their origin. It may not have been by accident that the first poem in the *Collected Poems, First Series*, prefaces the whole flight of 'joyful singing birds' by the admission that they come from brooding thunderstorms of the mind. It has not lain in the nature of this poet's genius to show us the gathering or dispersal of those storms; in these short lyrics it is only the mutter of the thunder that we hear when the storm is past. Perhaps we owe him the greater debt, for there are enough poets to do that and few not only to give us joy but to show us the cause of joy. Yet it is consoling to know that this joy is, at least in part, a deliberate joy. There are all the poems of accidental unexpected delight, but there are a few in which delight is consciously invited and even commanded; as in *The Owl*, where he vows in his 'final walk on earth' to make of the 'boding Owl's despair' 'a thing to fill my heart with mirth'. It may be suggested that, if Mr. Davies achieves this, he will do it, at any rate in part, by a kinship with those metaphysical poets of the seventeenth century who made themselves acquainted with Death by asking it riddles. The likeness is momentary rather than permanent; that is to say, it arises from particular experiences rather than from an effort after a universal philosophy. But it presents a poet's mind making a bearable and communicable thing of some intense moment of experience, otherwise almost unbearable. Mr. Davies has perhaps never been sufficiently praised for the intensity of his love-poetry, and it is there chiefly, if not entirely, that the likeness is seen. A poem called *A Maiden and her Hair* persuades the reader that some cancelled title must have read *To Anthea doing her Hair*. The last two stanzas must, and may, be sufficient to suggest that there is here the same kind of diction and rhythm by which the earlier poets could invest any action with a solemnity, significance, and (sometimes) hinted extreme of terror or peace.

> Sometimes one hand must fetch strange tools,
>   The other then must work alone;
> But when more instruments are brought,
>   See both make up the time that's gone.

> Now that her hair is bound secure,
>   Coil top of coil, in smaller space,
> Ah, now I see how smooth her brow,
>   And her simplicity of face.

The 'simplicity of face' of these poems has not yet prevented them from being attired with far comparisons and unexpected similes ('ten Isaiahs' souls'), nor from containing sudden epigrams of natural or social significance. For example, sparrows, it seems, fight as linnets and swallows do not, and perhaps it is as well to fight, like the poor, as to live

> In one long frozen state
> Of anger, like the great.

Or again, when the poet is stung by a wasp, he lets him go 'life-free'; if he had not, he says, it would have proved him only the stronger wasp.

It seems, then, that Mr. Davies's mind is extremely capable of receiving both complex and simple impressions, and those of both common and unusual sights, of universal and of rare experiences. There arises from these, since even merely 'staring' produces some effect on the mind, which is to be discerned in its next motion, a determination to accept and create Joy; a continued fresh surprise and delight in all things delectable, a deliberate dismissal of that side of things which so torments some of our modern poets, of fear and cruelty and the unhappiness of the common people. To do this needs a strength which is almost a virtue; its virtue in Mr. Davies is sufficiently proved by the strong and lovely things he has created. It is not sufficient to say that his poems exist in our minds like bird-marks in the snow; nor even that his mind opens in our own like 'a flowery, green, bird-singing land'—to do so is to underrate him. There is fire and food in these poems, and a shelter in the cold lands of the imagination. That he rather provides us with the bricks to build that shelter than builds it for us himself is due, no doubt, to the nature of his genius. But any reader who cares to meditate a little carefully on these poems will find in them an intensity and a universality which provide in themselves the 'depth' his critics desire. They have the three dimensions of nature, humanity, and thought, and they communicate everywhere that fourth dimension which we can only, rather helplessly, call poetry, and which causes us, in our turn and with a continually renewed admiration, to stand and stare.

End Piece

End Piece

Surprise sat on my window-sill,
    ah! I said, and *O!*
with a song my heart to fill;
    but did too soon go.
O'er the trees and through the skies
far beyond my aching eyes
went the wonder of surprise,
    that I once did know.

Wonder sat within my heart,
    ah! I said, and *O!*
but too soon it did depart,
    where I could not know.
Dear and lovely things are mine;
in my heart they glow and shine;
but that joy of wonder fine
    far away did go.

When I hear a poet's song,
    ah! I say, and *O!*
though I hear it oft and long
    wonder does not go;
for the holy poets still
with surprise my heart fulfil;
all my custom feels the thrill
    that I once did know.

WALTER DE LA MARE

Born 1873. He spent eighteen years in commercial life before, in 1908, devoting his time to literature. His first book (*Songs of Childhood*, 1901) was published under the name of Walter Ramal, but in 1904, for *Henry Brocken*, a prose romance, he used his own name. Before the *Collected Poems* (1920), his chief books of verse were *Poems* (1906), *A Child's Day* (1912), *The Listeners* (1912), *Peacock Pie* (1913), *Motley* (1918); and since then, *The Veil* (1921), *Down a Down Derry* (1922), *Ding Dong Bell* (1924). *Come Hither! an Anthology for the Young of all Ages* was published in 1923.

IF it were possible to distinguish in the work of poets between riches and richness, some such distinction might be held to separate Mr. de la Mare from his equals. The work of Hardy, Mr. Abercrombie, Mr. Chesterton, all has riches—in the sense that it all includes a large range of human experience, and that this experience is communicated, quintessentialized, in the verse. But the ruling idea or emotion in each case holds these other experiences within it, controls and directs and unifies them. It communicates itself by means of them; they are not lessened, but they are certainly tinged by it. But Mr. de la Mare's poetry seems, at first reading, to communicate nothing but itself. The poems may be about sorrow or death or love or any other emotional subject; the fact emerges, as it were, secondarily, from a richness which seems too beautiful to contain a mere intellectual significance.

If there were such a thing as 'pure poetry', or rather if what is meant by 'pure poetry' could be satisfying for very long, Mr. de la Mare would seem to be our greatest poet. But the phrase is ambiguous, and in certain relations suggests an emptying from verse of all intellectual and emotional significance other than its own. It excludes, that is to say, associated moods; moods which are rather recalled than expressed by the verse. When Mr. Chesterton, for example, brings in the name of some past hero of Christendom, he deliberately means to recall to us all that we know of him in myth or history:

> As to the Haut King came at morn
> Dead Roland on a doubtful horn,
> Seemed unto Alfred lightly borne
>   The last cry of the Gael.

It is, so far, 'impure' poetry—and none the less good for that; we need not impart any idea of superiority on one side or the other into the definition. But when Mr. de la Mare writes a poem about *The Great Alexander* he does implicitly dismiss from our minds all of the historic Alexander except royalty and conquest—Macedonia goes, and India, and Thais, and Darius; and it therefore approaches pure poetry. And when he abandons even such historic figures, and speaks only of the Queen Djenira—who, whether he got her name from some myth or from his own mind, is sufficiently unknown to most of us— he has to depend on, and we have to enjoy, merely what he can do with the name in the poem. And so with all his words. Pure poetry is that in which, from the common facts, the most general associations, is produced the most concentrated and piercing effect.[1]

[1] In the Conversation between Mr. de la Mare, Mr. John Freeman, and Mr. George Moore, which is the prelude to the anthology *Pure Poetry*, edited by Mr. Moore, 'pure poetry' is defined as 'something that the poet creates outside his own personality', and Mr. de la Mare appears to accept this. The definition is no

We are not, fortunately, confined to it, and forbidden to use for the noblest of human activities three-quarters of the furniture of our minds.

It is almost impossible not to compare Mr. de la Mare with Mr. Yeats. Of both poetries it is a temptation to use the word 'magical', for these two poets, more than any others living, are adept in the incantation through words of these indefinable emotions and unassociated passions. 'No—but opopanax and cinnamon;' what a satisfying line that is, yet its intellectual content is of the smallest! and Mr. de la Mare can do similar things. Both of them begin with faery—though with different realms of that world; both of them have moved into a world of profound humanity. But there the resemblance ceases. For it might be held that, though the reader derives an equally intense satisfaction from the later work of both poets, he receives from Mr. Yeats the communication of a rich and unappeased longing, while from Mr. de la Mare he receives a rich and appeased content. In Mr. Yeats's work there exists —a word may be borrowed from his own criticism— the 'antitype' of his desires, and from the half-loved, half-loathed encounter arise his moving lines. But Mr. de la Mare's work has neither type nor antitype; there is in it no vibrant conflict, and what conflict there is, is in it almost awfully subdued to a farther peace. There emerges from his verse the imagination at least of a state beyond Time.

doubt better than that given above, but both point to the same end, for it is by the particular associated moods which he calls up that a poet's personality is often indirectly made known. And certainly both definitions exclude doctrine and formulated ideas.

A number of these poems, nevertheless, are about things that imply conflict—fear and parting and madness, and even more evil possibilities. A number of them again are about death. But it is not death understood, as it is normally understood by most of us, as a state devoid of experience and empty of realization. Whatever our intellectual beliefs may be, the word death generally suggests a 'naughting' of all that we know. We may expect to know other things and even dimly hope to know lovelier; but such expectation and hope are slender emotions. In Mr. de la Mare's poems there is a state of removed ecstasy; it is as though death had become, not a gate to experience, but itself a rich experience, a summing-up and transcending of all present beauty and richness. It is removed in two senses; first, it is—as it must be in poetry—not something to be looked forward to in time and with the natural mind, but to be felt here and with the 'holy imagination' which Blake perceived to be the Saviour of men; it is therefore something more removed than a promise, being a state which exists already within us, but into which we have not entered. And secondly, it is a state which is beyond, and beyond in the sense of including, those other experiences of fear and mistake and terror These, which are separate poems, are elements of the whole; transforming these into beauty, Mr. de la Mare has persuaded us of an inclusive ecstasy.

In this most passionate verse there is one thing perhaps lacking, and yet it seems ungracious to speak of it. If it is spoken of at all, it must be not in complaint or regret but merely as a warning to some readers. Not even Mr. de la Mare can give us everything, and the thing he has not condescended to give us is philosophy. This statement implies no pride on his part, but it does imply that this beauty will not of itself shape itself in metaphysical thought, or anyhow not in rationalized metaphysical thought. The emotion is too intense, it seems, to do so, yet some such modification might be a relief. It is, normally, when the intensity of emotion no longer exists that we turn to thought, or perhaps the turning is itself a natural lowering of the emotion. Normally, but not necessarily; certain great and passionate minds have had intellect as well as feeling enlarged and influenced. But that hardly happens here—though such a phrase should be modified with all the 'perhapses' possible. For it is, by whatever road he has reached it, from *beyond* thought that this communication comes, and thought in itself could never find the way to know it.

That Mr. de la Mare could have dealt with metaphysics if he had chosen is suggested by at any rate two or three of the earlier poems, as, for example, *Poor Jim Jay*, a metaphysical fairy-tale.

> Do diddle di do,
>   Poor Jim Jay
> Got stuck fast
>   In Yesterday ...
> We pulled and we pulled
>   From seven till twelve,
> Jim, too frightened
>   To help himself.
> But all in vain.
>   The clock struck one,
> And there was Jim

> A little bit gone.
> At half-past five
> You scarce could see
> A glimpse of his flapping
> Handkerchee ...

This is an extreme example, because here the subject of the poem is very much less a simple fact than is usual with Mr. de la Mare. It seems ridiculous to say of a poet who has been admired so generally for his fantastic or faery poems that he is in those poems always concerned with facts, and yet it seems to be true. For in poetry (it is the first rule in the book) we need not concern ourselves with the question whether a fact is a fact in the phenomenal world or not. A poem which begins

> There were two Fairies, Gimmul and Mel,

deals as much with a fact as that other which begins

> Thick in its glass
> The physic stands.

A reader has of course the right to say he is not interested in one set of facts, as he has to refuse to be concerned with, say, electricity, economics, or biology, and then there can be no further discussion. But if there is to be, we must accept all a poet's facts, and it is then that we discover the extreme simplicity and yet the multitudinousness of Mr. de la Mare's approaches to them. In a quatrain which appears to one reader as an immortal simplicity of English verse, he has said—

> It's a very odd thing
> As odd as can be
> That whatever Miss T. eats
> Turns into Miss T.

This stands with such other simplicities as Donne's

> I wonder, by my troth, what thou and I
> Did till we loved;

or the anonymous

> When Molly smiles beneath her cow
> I feel my heart I can't tell how.

It is the astonishing *fact* that holds all three poets in amazed entrancement. The surprise is not, in Mr. de la Mare, the thing that is always most immediately communicated by his verse; he has many ways of approach, but it is always the central fact that he concerns himself with, in the moods of lyric verse, or the statements of narrative. His goblins and fairies, moons and queens, Arabia and England, are accompaniments and definitions. But, with those few exceptions which show us he could have dealt with philosophy if he had chosen, this fact is one of the emotions with which in ordinary life we are most generally acquainted—sorrow and hope and ardour and anger and their like; and others —more rare and more intense than they—terror, and the desire for rest, and ecstasy. In some of 'the old wisdoms' of which Mr. Yeats has spoken, ecstasy was to be experienced in the magical trance, and, so far as Mr. de la Mare can be called a 'magical' poet, it is because he throws us half into a trance with his incantations.

In the poem which closes *Peacock Pie* he achieves one of the most remarkable effects in modern verse.

The Song of Finis

At the edge of All the Ages
  A Knight sate on his steed,
His armour red and thin with rust,
  His soul from sorrow freed;
And he lifted up his visor
  From a face of skin and bone,
And his horse turned head and whinnied
  As the twain stood there alone.

No bird above that steep of time
  Sang of a livelong quest;
No wind breathed,
    Rest:
'Lone for an end!' cried Knight to steed,
  Loosed an eager rein—
Charged with his challenge into Space:
  And quiet did quiet remain.

'And quiet did quiet remain.' We are—to put it clumsily—*there* even to experience that quiet, and yet we are *not* there; nothing is there. The single image has vanished into space; we are, for a moment, in a state beyond images, and therefore beyond intellect. Poetry has many ways of doing this, but it rarely does it so simply and finally as here. And yet that quiet, if it is not broken by, is at any rate achieved after, other states as rare and as rarely communicated. There is, for example, in one or two poems, even of these earlier ones, something inexplicably sinister; as in *Jemima* or *The Mocking Fairy*. It may be a merely personal temperament that finds those two poems—the first slightly, the second altogether—terrifying. In this world of facts what dreadful fact expresses something of itself in the poem about Mrs. Gill?

The Mocking Fairy

'Won't you look out of your window, Mrs. Gill?'
   Quoth the Fairy, nidding, nodding in the garden,
'*Can't* you look out of your window, Mrs. Gill?'
   Quoth the Fairy, laughing softly in the garden;
But the air was still, the cherry boughs were still,
And the ivy-tod neath the empty sill,
And never from her window looked out Mrs. Gill
   On the Fairy shrilly mocking in the garden.

'What have they done with you, you poor Mrs. Gill?'
   Quoth the Fairy brightly glancing in the garden;
'Where have they hidden you, you poor old Mrs. Gill?'
   Quoth the Fairy dancing lightly in the garden;
But night's faint veil now wrapped the hill,
Stark 'neath the stars stood the dead-still Mill,
And out of her cold cottage never answered Mrs. Gill
   The Fairy mimbling mambling in the garden.

Why is that Fairy so dreadful? 'Quiet did quiet remain.' Was Mrs. Gill dead? and did the Fairy know it? Obviously; but the mere indirectness of the communicated fact increases the terror. And what joy of non-human malice lay behind that mockery?

So in *Jemima*—the child whose father and mother always call her 'Meg', though her name is Jemima:

> Only my sister, jealous of
>   The strands of my bright hair,
> 'Jemima-mima-mima'
>   Calls, mocking, up the stair.

It is childish malice and childish mockery, but the childishness does not lessen the mockery and malice, and the cry pursues us up the stair into the higher towers of this house of verse.

These earlier poems deal with facts, of the world of phenomena or the world of fairy and romance. They deal with them directly, they deck them with actual or fantastic details, they wake in the reader either a surprised and delightful recognition—as in the poem about Miss T.—which is kin to ecstasy, or a surrender to some rare emotion. In some of them there is an intense expectation; something is just about to happen—and it might seem an unfair limitation of Mr. de la Mare's genius if we complained that nothing ever does happen. It has not happened *in* the poems; it has happened *to* the poems. Astonishingly and secretly those poems of surprise and fantasy have vanished before poems in which exterior fact has disappeared almost altogether. Turning, as it were, to the emotions which it has itself evoked, Mr. de la Mare's poetry has made them its subjects and penetrated farther and farther into the dim and rich world of our less-defined desires. If all theological connotation, all dogma, all ordinary piety, could be emptied out of the word religion, then this poetry might be called religious poetry. If the word mystical were not used nowadays for every cheap sensation and every indolent thought, it might almost be called mystical poetry; and if magic could ever lead to mysticism one would be tempted to say it had done so here. In an unnatural and fascinating labour we might even attempt to arrange these poems in some order of their soft movement from state to state of that little-explored world.

They have made their progress in sadness and

terror, but they have believed passionately and their passion has not failed them. Here and there are poems created by some horror in the actual world—*Drugged* and *In the Dock*, for example. There are others in which the idea of nothingness recurs. The titmouse, in one,

> into time's enormous nought,
> Sweet-fed, will flit away.

And in a most beautiful poem called *The Tryst*, the poet's imagination, after playing—almost sorrowfully—with some dream of a place of peace—

> Seek we some close hid shadow for our lair,
> Hollowed by Noah's mouse beneath the chair
> Wherein the Omnipotent, in slumber bound,
> Nods till the piteous Trump of Judgement sound—

and again:

> Think! in Time's smallest clock's minutest beat
> Might there not rest be found for wandering feet?—

concludes,

> No, No. Nor earth, nor air, nor fire, nor deep
> Could lull poor mortal longingness asleep.
> Somewhere there Nothing is; and there lost Man
> Shall win what changeless vague of peace he can.

It cannot be merely by an accident that Nothing occurs so frequently in contemporary poets. Hardy, Mr. Housman, Mr. Yeats, Mr. de la Mare— 'Somewhere there Nothing is'; somewhere consciousness shall cease, the first two might assure us. But the others have spoken rather of a transmuted consciousness. *Where there is Nothing there is God*, Mr. Yeats called one of his plays; and Mr. de la

Mare's poetry has charged that Nothing with beauty
and significance. Adam in one poem says

> Oh, from wide circuit, shall at length I see
> Pure daybreak lighten again on Eden's tree?
> Loosed from remorse and hope and love's distress,
> Enrobe me again in my lost nakedness?
> No more with wordless grief a loved one grieve,
> But to heaven's nothingness re-welcome Eve?

There are dangers enough in the way; there is a
poem, *The Monologue*, which begins

> Alas, O Lovely One,
>   Imprisoned here,
> I tap; thou answerest not,
>   I doubt and fear;

and ends:

> Long hours there are,
>   When mutely tapping—well,
> Is it to Vacancy
>   I these tidings tell?
> Knock these numb fingers against
>   An empty cell?
>
> Nay, answer not.
>   Let still mere longing make
> Thy presence sure to me,
>   While in doubt I shake:
> Be but my Faith in thee,
>   For sanity's sake.

It is such things as the use of the phrase 'O Lovely
One' that help to keep Mr. de la Mare's verse in the
region of what is unsatisfactorily called 'pure poetry'.
In some poets the appeal might have been to God;
in some to an abstract Beauty; in some to poetry

itself. But the associations of such words are not allowed to enter this poetry—or very rarely. There are a very few poems in which Mr. de la Mare addresses himself to a 'personal' God, and a few others in which he speaks of some apparently absent Power as if of a Person—but they come very infrequently. As in the earlier poems he preferred common things and fantastic things, England and Arabia, Little Henry and the Queen Djenira, so here he prefers to speak of such common things as sleep and sorrow and despair, or of such significant fantasies as Paradise and the 'Lovely One', and the sea-maids, and the states known in them are known in poetry.

Such a method has its dangers. When doctrine, and with doctrine intellect, is subdued entirely to emotional desire; when the very desired end itself is called Nothing; when in some poems the communication is of a state in which our mere existence would destroy its calm—then it is almost inevitable that the music sometimes should seem to quiver with the void rather than with peace. There are times when it seems too removed, too thin, too empty, for our enjoyment. Such a mood in the reader is as inevitable as are, in the history of criticism, those continual revolts against the princes of a past generation, of which the latest—against the great Victorians—is drawing to a close. Mr. de la Mare is fortunate if he suffers such a revolt in his lifetime, for then his reputation will be safe. In the ever-expanding greatness of English verse it is improbable that more than a score or so of these poems will continue to be generally known; the rest will be reserved for the British Museum Library, special editions, and a few devotees in every generation. But among those will be some of the most beautiful lyrics in English, a new expression of our secular desire; and among them also, let us hope, some of the entire simplicities of the earlier books. For, when all is said, and 'time's enormous nought' reckoned with, on the very edge of that state 'where quiet does quiet remain', it still is a very odd thing,

> And as odd as can be,
> That whatever Miss T. eats
> Turns into Miss T.

End Piece

End Piece

The Muse unlatched her window
    and looked from her faerie hold
on all the flowing silence
    that does her towers enfold;
quiet so quiet, through low and high,
there is no sound to measure it by.

Within were the strong romances,
    chapels and wars and songs,
Chaucer talking to Dryden,
    and all the poets' throngs,
but without through the hush fell the Muse's sigh—
where nothing is and nothing goes by.

The Muse unlatched a window;
    all that was said or sung
came to her still remembrance
    in the lovely English tongue,
but from a small window, very high,
she saw the silence flowing by.

Within were solitudes many
    and poetry's roaring gales,
Milton in meditation,
    and magic and faerie tales;
but knowledge had only the Muse's sigh
to measure the outer stillness by.

GILBERT KEITH CHESTERTON

Born 1874. He attended art classes at the Slade School, and has illustrated several books (mostly novels by Mr. Belloc). But he soon turned to journalism, and for a long while his Saturday column in the *Daily News* was—to many young readers—the most exciting event of the week. He was one of the leaders of the attack on the party system which was developing before the war, and since the war he has become the leader of the Distributist Movement in politics and economics—a movement which endeavours to provide a social method other than capitalism and socialism. His poetry consists of *The Wild Knight* (1905), *The Ballad of the White Horse* (1913); *Poems* (1915); *The Ballad of St. Barbara* (1925); *Collected Poems* (1927); *The Queen of the Seven Swords* (1927).

OF all the modern poets there is only one whose verse is always full of the voice of battle, and that is Mr. Chesterton. In the *Dynasts*, though we watch Trafalgar and Leipsic and Waterloo, it is from a height too far removed to hear the sound of the charges and the cannon, and Hardy has seen to it that the song or shout of victory shall be thin and paltry enough in our ears. But Mr. Chesterton's verse, even when it is not concerned with historic battles —Ethandune, Lepanto, the Marne—has generally the sound of a battle within it. There are drawn swords from the first page to the last, material, intellectual, and spiritual; the swords of Arthur and Roland, of Ben Tillett and Paul Deroulède, of the Mother of God and Michael the Archangel. Everything is spoken of in terms of war, either actual or potential. For even when there is no enemy the state of being described is a state where man is strung to a high pitch of expectation and his delight is already militant. The babe unborn in one poem looks forward to 'leave to weep and fight', and his old men die either in conflict or in the joy or fear of conflict. Man must be either a hero or a coward.

If it were not that the vocabulary of this poet is in itself so largely taken from battle and the things of battle, it would be sufficient to say that his verse always seems to be dealing with a crisis. But all poetry, in its nature, tends to deal with crises, either for their accentuation or resolution; and this more universal word scarcely fits so well the part which man himself takes, according to Mr. Chesterton's poetry, in the resolution of the critical moment. Here, if anywhere in English verse, he is a fighting animal, and here he is scarcely anything else. Whether that dream in which he has seen himself and his affairs as important be true or false, the knowledge of a mystic or the rationalizing of a madman, it is certainly as important that he appears here. Mr. Chesterton and Mr. Housman hold up between them all the philosophies; man conquers or he endures.

To speak of Milton in this connexion would seem absurd—for Mr. Chesterton's theology is as Catholic (in the Roman sense of the word) as Milton's was Puritan, his politics as democratic as Milton's were aristocratic, and his sense of enjoyment as universal as Milton's was ascetic; and yet there is perhaps no English poetry which in the matter of combat Mr. Chesterton's verse so much resembles. Both these poets deal with the combat in its cosmic, mundane, and localized forms, and as Milton conducted (ostensibly, at any rate) campaigns against Satan, the Philistines, the Bishops, and the King of England, so Mr. Chesterton has attacked the Dragon, the Danes, the Turks, the Prohibitionists, and Lord Birkenhead. Both of them have fought for definite and enunciable principles. Both of them, though rarely, have suggested in the middle of their warlike and triumphant verse the state which is beyond warfare, and which opens upon the soul when, and whether, the last battle has been won or lost. It might almost be added that neither of them has felt, or at any rate has allowed himself to express, what his opponent really wanted; but the charge could hardly be sustained. For Milton has been accused for generations of understanding only too well what Satan wanted; and it is certain that some of Mr. Chesterton's opponents know less clearly even than he for what intellectual end they are striving.

All the magnificent imagery of forlorn hopes and last charges and final stands and broken swords which Mr. Chesterton has strewn about his poems does not conceal the fact that he is, on the whole, on the side of the big battalions. Nor would he desire to conceal it; on the contrary, he asserts it—it is his claim and his song throughout. He is on the side of God and the people. But, in a sense, both of his great allies are voiceless and unarmed. It is he who is their song and weapon; and his weapon is his song. It is always the few whom he attacks, but it is the few in possession, the pseudo-scientists, the politicians, the usurers, King Dives. In this large simplification it is probable enough that he seems to do a good deal of injustice. It is probable that the people will not always be grateful for what he offers them, and that (for example) a good deal of spurious democracy and comfortably-vicarious combativeness may strengthen themselves on these noble poems. But that is not his business. And as against that, the lucidity of some of the topical poems can be appreciated by minds which are far enough from the causes for which he stands. It is not necessary to have an opinion on the Welsh Disestablishment Bill to appreciate the folly of the remark that it 'had shocked the conscience of every Christian community in Europe', which gave rise to the famous *Antichrist, or the Reunion of Christendom: an Ode.* Nor need one be in obedience to Rome to appreciate the worth of that negligible periodical which claimed that the Church of Rome was troubled by the opposition of Sir Arthur Conan Doyle and Mr. Dennis Bradley—

> If she must lean on lesser props
> Of earthly fame or ancient art,
> Make shift with Raphael and Racine
> Put up with Dante and Descartes,
> Not wholly can she blind her grief,
> But touch the wound and murmur sadly,
> 'These lesser things are theirs to love
> Who lose the love of Mr. Bradley'.

And there are other things of the same kind. These things, poems and provocations alike, have their place in the gaiety of the created universe.

These poems, however, are not Mr. Chesterton's most important, however dearly they may be loved. Nor, merely because of their shattering rightness, is there felt in them that combination of the forlorn hope and the big battalions which gives quite peculiar force to some of the others. It derives, at least in part, from that tradition and creed of Christendom to which Mr. Chesterton's entire genius and loyalty has been devoted: the creed of God crucified. But it is strengthened by the fact that some such paradox is discoverable in the world everywhere. The Incarnation and the Passion recur everywhere in this poetry. But there recurs also the poetic sense of the danger in which single and helpless things stand—and this is the correlation of the one, as the general struggle, and especially that struggle in which defeat is practically certain, is the correlation of the other. For one of the facts that makes the combination of which we have spoken possible is simply that the big battalions are made up of an infinite number of forlorn hopes. Few things have occurred to bigger battalions of men than, for instance, romantic love. But the sense of it is universal because it is individual. And to each experience Mr. Chesterton implicitly attributes such apocalyptic values, and casts about it a rain of such gigantic terms, that it takes on the appearance of an ultimate romantic war.

> Little I reck of empty prides,
>   Of creeds more cold than clay;
> To nobler ends and longer rides
>   My lady rides to-day.
> To swing our swords and take our sides
>   In that all-ending fray
> When stars fall down and darkness hides,
>   When God shall turn to bay.

There has never been a poet who took sides more vigorously than Mr. Chesterton. 'God turning to bay' is the continual theme of this verse—it occurred in the *Napoleon of Notting Hill*, published years before—but it is a proof of its integrity that the phrase does not, as so easily it might, become a mere stupid reiteration. Some have held it to be blasphemy—as in Walt Whitman's lines:

Silent and amazed even when a little boy,
I remember I heard the preacher every Sunday put God in his statements,
As contending against some being or influence—

but to Mr. Chesterton it has been the centre of poetic life, and it is for the sake of that tradition that he has spent so much energy on insisting that nothing worth having is to be gained by a false unity,

>When man is the Turk and the Atheist,
>Essene, Erastian Whig,
>And the Thug and the Druse and the Catholic
>And the crew of the Captain's gig.

(But it is, of course, possible to believe that the seven types named—and others—are, precisely, the crew of the Captain's gig.)

But all these poems of war and battle, all this sympathy with the weak and suffering, all this defiance of the rich and learned, all this wit and humour and theology and traditionalism—does it after all make poetry? In the sense that it is all part of the Muse's preoccupation, all part of the things that she can and must do, it is as much poetry as Pope's attack on Addison or Shelley's couplet on Castlereagh; and it will be unfortunate if poetry is ever so limited as to omit such admirable labours. Nevertheless, they are rather her indulgences than her life. They are not of the nature of her great achievements; they are collateral, not direct, inheritors of her kingdom. And before considering the finest poems something should be said about the disadvantage of Mr. Chesterton's style.

There are moments, especially when it is the volume of *Collected Poems* which one reads, when one is defeated by the mere noise of the thing. Both artistically and spiritually one is exhausted by the continual crying of the trumpet, by the shouting and staring colours, by the sunsets, the sunrises, the crashing heavens, the incalculable abysses, the scarlet and gold and brass, 'unthinkable wings', 'stairs of hell', 'white web of splendour', 'battles unborn and vast', 'drink to the wrath of God', and a thousand other catastrophes. There are quiet poems, but they are so few, and even they are held in the midst of a strained and everlasting vigilance. May the reader never be at peace? If the Muse must ride like St. Joan, might she not sometimes dream, happily and simply, of Domrémy?

She has not dreamed; she has sometimes had nightmares, but not of Domrémy. When she has remembered the places of childhood and the golden world it has been not with wistfulness, or delight, or simplicity, or longing, as in so many poets, but with the same surprise with which she first saw them. Mr. Chesterton has said in one poem (and the statement is borne out by many others):

> Behold, the crowning mercies melt,
>   The first surprises stay;
> And in my dross is dropped a gift
>   For which I dare not pray:
> That a man grow used to grief and joy
>   But not to night and day.
>
> A thrill of thunder in my hair;
>   Though blackening clouds be plain,

> Still I am stung and startled
>   By the first drop of the rain:
> Romance and pride and passion pass
>   And these are what remain.
>
> Strange crawling carpets of the grass,
>   Wide windows of the sky.
> So in this perilous grace of God
>   With all my sins go I:
> And things grow new though I grow old,
>   Though I grow old and die.

Notable as, in the general decay which attacks men, this single continual resurrection is, it has to be admitted that it accentuates the noise of the verse. Between the shouts of surprise and the shouts of war the reader spurs for home and peace.

He may find it in certain other poems, even though they also are of war, in *Lepanto*, in *Saint Barbara*, in *The Ballad of the White Horse*; especially in the last, which is not only Mr. Chesterton's finest poem, but in itself one of the greatest of modern poems. For in these three poems the outward battles of Lepanto and the Marne and Ethandune are assumed into the inner conflict. They are no mere historic poems, nor merely expressions of the Catholic and democratic tradition against the Mahommedans, the Prussians, or the Danes, they penetrate more and more deeply into that state of being which is common to humanity when every man feels that he is indeed fighting forlornly, in a cause which he hardly knows and in which he does not believe, against spiritual enemies and interior treacheries who are triumphant and all but omnipotent. It answers to that state which is communicated in Mr. Housman's verse; it is all but final, and indeed at the moment when it exists it appears final. But in this verse that state is changed from within; there arise upon the world victory and the renewal of common things.

Of the three poems which have been mentioned *Lepanto* has least to do with this change. It is one of Mr. Chesterton's greatest artistic successes, with the various long stanzas dealing with the great figures, historical or traditional—the Soldan, Mahomet, St. Michael, King Philip, the Pope—and the varying refrain describing the passing of Don John of Austria through Europe to the battle and his victory there. It is true that the thrill of the stanza describing the setting free of the Christian captives in the galleys is a little spoiled for those readers who remember Motley's estimate that at least 7,200 Turkish slaves were distributed among the Christian princes (Don John himself receiving 174 as a present from the Pope). But it would be unfair to allow the historical fact—if it is a fact—to spoil one's pleasure in a poem which is a romantic expression of a romantic abandonment to emotion. It is much more to the point to remember the last stanza of all, in which, after the magnificent lines describing the battle, there comes a reminder of the roads of a peaceful land and of the unfathomable irony of Cervantes.

Cervantes on his galley sets the sword back in the sheath,
(*Don John of Austria rides homeward with a wreath,*)
And he sees across a weary land a straggling road in Spain,
Up which a lean and foolish knight forever rides in vain,

And he smiles, but not as Sultans smile, and settles back the
    blade . . .
(*But Don John of Austria rides home from the Crusade*).

Saint Barbara, however, goes beyond this in its communication of experience. In the first place it is a story of the First Battle of the Marne, and therefore of all but ultimate defeat preceding victory. The legend of the saint is told by a Breton to a Norman, in the moment which precedes the opening of the Allied cannonade and the charge of Europe, and the tale of martyrdom is interrupted by the murmur of endurance.

They are firing, we are falling, and the red skies rend and
    shiver us.
Barbara, Barbara, we may not loose a breath—
Be at the bursting doors of doom and in the dark deliver us
Who loosen the last window on the sun of sudden death.

All through the poem the word 'windows' runs like something more than a refrain. 'Ruin is a builder of windows'. The face of St. Barbara was 'like a window

    where a man's first love looked out'.

She is shut up in a tower which has two windows only, and in it she breaks open a third.

    —out of the third lattice under low eaves like wings
    Is a new corner of the sky and the other side of things.

There is peace between Caesar and all the gods,

But not with the three windows and the third name of god.

And it recurs again in the great climax of victory to which the poem rises

They are stopped and gapped and battered as we blast away the weather
Building window upon window to our lady of the light.

Blast of the beauty of sudden death, St. Barbara of the batteries!
That blow the new white window in the wall of all the world.

But he that told the tale went home to his house beside the sea
And burned before St. Barbara, the light of the windows three;
Three candles for an unknown thing, never to come again,
That opened like the eye of God on Paris in the plain.

The finest lines, perhaps, in a poem which would be a fantasy if it were not made real by so strong a sense of disaster and death, are those which seem for an instant to catch something of the supernatural light it speaks of.

What light upon what ancient way shines to a far-off floor,
The line of the lost land of France or the plains of Paradise?

It is through the third window that the one is seen to be indeed the other, through the window of ruin or sudden death, in the moment most hopeless of earth and heaven, that earth and heaven are seen to be miraculously one.

The longest and greatest poem of all, *The Ballad of the White Horse*, is, as it should be, the completest. It is the story of Alfred the King in hiding, in battle, and in victory; of the friends, the Saxon, the Celt, and the Roman—the three traditions of the English —who are called to his aid; and of the fable of the cakes. There is nowhere a more complete statement of Mr. Chesterton's creed, or of his philosophy, nor anywhere a more complete communication of it by experience rather than by mere statement. One reviewer, when it first appeared, wrote that there had been no better fighting since Homer, but though this seems true enough (witness the magnificent stanzas which rehearse the names of those whom the King slays), it is not for this that it is remembered. The reader can enjoy that as he does a joke, or the roll of names in Shakespeare, Milton, or Mr. Kipling; his 'enjoyment' of the poem as a whole must be more profound. It begins with an account of those days when

> There was death on the Emperor,
>   And night upon the Pope,
> And Alfred, hiding in deep grass,
>   Hardened his heart with hope—

the last line of which stanza is an example of Mr. Chesterton's mastery of epigram; in this also he confronts Mr. Housman almost alone of modern poets. In those days the only message which the King receives from a vision of the Mother of God, and carries to his friends, is that

> the sky grows darker yet,
> And the sea rises higher.

Afterwards he goes—as in the old tale—to the Danish camp and sings there, and there also the Danish chiefs and Guthrum the King himself sing. In those five songs five 'judgements on life' are delivered, five different creeds express themselves. And it is not the smallest praise of this poem that Mr.

Chesterton has here done what he has not always cared to do, and expressed those creeds with a complete understanding. Not Hardy himself has sung of the evil chances of life more poignantly:

> There is always a thing forgotten
> When all the world goes well...
>
> The thing on the blind side of the heart,
> On the wrong side of the door,
> The green plant groweth, menacing
> Almighty lovers in the spring,
> There is always a forgotten thing,
> And love is not secure.

And, though it is expressed plaintively rather than strongly, Guthrum's own song carries something of the *Shropshire Lad's* sadness.

> The little brooks are very sweet
> Like a girl's ribbons curled,
> But the great sea is bitter
> That washes all the world.

For whatever philosophy a man holds to, he is bound to admit all the others—if only as moods, and they are so admitted here and expressed. Alfred's own strength lies in three things, a belief that the universe is just, a willingness to work simply and naturally at the thing before him—whether within or without—and a capacity for laughter at himself. When he has been struck by the woman whose cakes he has let burn while he brooded over the hard lot of all the working world, he stands with torture 'and the evil things'

> That are in the childish hearts of kings
> An instant in his eyes.

Then he breaks into a giant laughter, and in the midst of that laughter he heads the march on the Danes.

The battle is all but lost; Alfred with his Saxon and Roman following is beaten one way, and the Celts (their leader Colan slain) another. He rallies the few that are left him.

> And when the last arrow
>   Was fitted and was flown,
> When the broken shield hung on the breast
> And the hopeless lance was laid in rest,
>   And the hopeless horn blown,
>
> The King looked up . . .

at an instant's vision again of the Mother of God. There follows the last victorious charge, and with a wonderful and perhaps unpremeditated effect of the intrusion of unreasonable and supernatural things, the Celts also break into the battle.

> And highest sang the slaughter,
>   And fastest fell the slain,
> When from the wood-road's blackening throat
> A crowning and crashing wonder smote
>   The rear-guard of the Dane.
>
> For the dregs of Colan's company—
>   Lost down the other road—
> Had gathered and grown and heard the din,
> And with wild yells came pouring in,
> Naked as their old British kin,
>   And bright with blood for woad.
>
> And bare and bloody and aloft
>   They bore before their band
> The body of their mighty lord,
> Colan of Caerleon and its horde,

That bore King Alfred's battle-sword
　　Broken in his left hand.

And a strange music went with him,
　　Loud and yet strangely far;
The wild pipes of the western land,
Too keen for the ear to understand,
Sang high and deathly on each hand
　　When the dead man went to war.

Blocked between ghost and buccaneer,
　　Brave men have dropped and died;
And the wild sea-lords well might quail
As the ghastly war-pipes of the Gael
Called to the horns of White Horse Vale,
　　And all the horns replied.

There is no section of the poem which has not its vignettes—of history, or nature, or common life, or philosophy. The march of Eldred and his farm-hands, the Roman tradition, the basis of all monogamy, the description of a medieval manuscript, of the forest disturbed by Alfred's march, of the courts to which his embassies go, all these and many things like them are given in a stanza or two. It is one of those poems which are rich in human experience, and these riches combine with a sense of the ultimate moment of despair and its transmutation to make it the great thing it undoubtedly is. The apocalyptic and cosmic imagery is reduced to as little as is possible with Mr. Chesterton, and the very setting of the poem in those days of the Dark Ages seems to justify what there is. 'Caesar's sun fell out of the sky', and in that darkness the enormous things that moved may very well have enormous comparisons to express them.

In the midst, then, of poetry which seems to express nothing but war, in the midst of topical jokes and topical satires, of a shouted surprise and a roaring combativeness, there arises this sense of peace. Mr. Chesterton has been called an optimist and a medievalist and many other things. But it is because the things for which he has fought, carelessly considered, have a certain superficial resemblance to what is usually meant by those carelessly employed terms. It is, in fact, impossible to describe one of the finest poets of our time so easily. His verse certainly need not pray to be delivered

>   From all the easy speeches
>   That comfort cruel men.

He has no hope of gratitude from the people:

>   For we are for all men under the sun,
>   And they are against us, every one.

It is in the hour of defeat that he, like Alfred, is most himself.

> The line breaks, and the guns go under,
>   The lords and the lackeys ride the plain,
> And I draw deep breaths of the dawn and thunder
>   And the whole of my heart grows young again . . .
>   For we that fight till the world is free
>   We are not easy in victory,
>   We have known each other too long, my brother,
>   And fought each other, the world and we.

End Piece

End Piece

About the house of Dives
   the laws and lictors stand
and all the starving people
   are driven at his command:
upon an ordered nation
   his servants' eyes look down—
but the Crown is still in exile,
   and the people are the Crown.

Across the thronging markets
   they build his flowering arch,
and Dives' younger brother
   hath led the rebels' march,
wherefore King Dives triumphs
   whichever flag go down—
but the Crown is still in exile,
   and the people are the Crown.

The Muse that gave Prometheus
   to Shelley's eager glance,
The Muse that cried to Wordsworth
   among the fields of France,
have we forgot their chorus
   beneath King Dives' frown?—
for the Crown is still in exile
   and the people are the Crown.

But still in hidden alleys
   the holy child is born
and still in open judgement
   his freedom wears the thorn;
for Caiaphas and Herod
   and Pilate sway the town—
while the Crown is still in exile
   and the people are the Crown.

JOHN MASEFIELD

Mr. Masefield has kept his biography—deliberately—as far as possible to himself. It is said that he was born in 1876, went to sea at an early age, spent years in adventures by sea and land, and afterwards returned to England and devoted himself to literature. His first book was *Salt Water Ballads* (1902); his first famous book in verse was *The Everlasting Mercy* (1911), and was followed by *The Widow in the Bye Street* (1912), *Dauber* (1913), *The Daffodil Fields* (1913). *Reynard the Fox* appeared in 1919 (other volumes having occupied the interval), and *Right Royal* in 1920. The *Collected Poems* appeared in 1923.

In the first line of the first poem of his *Collected Poems* Mr. Masefield announces that he is not concerned with 'the princes and prelates with periwigged charioteers', and indeed the word 'periwig' suggests at once all that is most opposite to his verse. Of all centuries Mr. Masefield seems to have least to do with the eighteenth, with that superb effort towards control and stability which was common to Pope and Johnson and Gibbon. The overmastering, and yet overmastered, passion of that great couplet—

Poets themselves must fall like those they sung;
Deaf the praised ear and mute the tuneful tongue—

is of a kind of verse which Mr. Masefield has hardly ever essayed. An older, though not a greater, poet is his brother in the Muse; the patron of his style is Edmund Spenser.

Spenser, with his knights and enchanters and witches and paynims, his hermitages and palaces, his lonely champions and complex pageantries, his allegories and morals, Gloriana and Britomart? Spenser—when Mr. Masefield wants to sing of the working man, 'the sailor, the stoker of steamers, the man with the clout'? But subject is not the only thing that makes up poetry; though, if it were, there would still be a likeness between Mr. Masefield's continual invocations of Beauty and Spenser's *Hymns*. The background of verbiage out of which the poet appears must count for something. No poet yet has succeeded in leaving that background entirely behind him; however far he comes, we can still see the ways by which he emerges from mere language into ordered speech. These backgrounds and avenues have sometimes the most probable, sometimes the most improbable likenesses. There is Marlowe behind Shakespeare, and Keats behind Tennyson. But there is also Pope behind Patmore, and the Elizabethans behind Pope.

The most fascinating thing about Mr. Masefield is this appearance of an expansive romanticism. If there were nothing else, the modern poet's work would be almost a joke; but there is sufficient of something else to make us interested in the contrast. But that something is not what Mr. Masefield insisted upon in that 'Consecration' of his first book, *Salt Water Ballads*. It was not when the book was published in 1902; it has certainly not been since. Ordinary men, working men, 'the drowsy man at the wheel and the tired look-out', come in from time to time. But they come mostly, for all their modern properties, down those old Spenserian ways, those lengthy, twining roads, where even fights are drowsy, and crises are resolved into faery by the mere process of time. Outside Spenser, was ever a fight so melodious a business as this?

> 'We do not stop till one of us is dead,'
> Said Lion, rushing in. A short blow fell

Dizzily, through all guard, on Michael's head.
His hedging-hook slashed blindly but too well:
It struck in Lion's side. Then, for a spell,
Both, sorely stricken, staggered, while their eyes
Dimmed under mists of blood; they fell, they tried to rise,—

Tried hard to rise, but could not, so they lay,
Watching the clouds go sailing on the sky,
Touched with a redness from the end of day.
There was all April in the blackbird's cry.
And lying there they felt they had to die,
Die and go under mould and feel no more
April's green fire of life go running in earth's core.

. . . .

He tilted up the hat, and Lion drank.
Lion lay still a moment, gathering power,
Then rose, as Michael gave him more, and sank.
Then, like a dying bird whom death makes tower,
He raised himself above the bloodied flower
And struck with all his force in Michael's side.
'You should not have done that,' his stricken comrade cried.

'You should not have done that'—the reader involuntarily assents. He shouldn't, of course; it was bad manners. But paynims do behave badly; it is why they are there at all. And Mr. Masefield's paynims—outside their official paynimry—are all the gentlest people; they are the properties of an exterior romanticism.

The romantic mind is that which wholly abandons itself to some intense experience, and normally does not stabilize that by others. But this is the interior and greater romanticism. There exists also a lesser kind which has the trappings of that greater romance without its intensity. The decorations of death, the ornamentations of love, hide the thing itself, and sometimes hide it very beautifully. The substitution may be rich and lovely, but it is a substitution. Spenser, in *The Faerie Queene*, is full of it; the whole poem is a substitution of loveliness for intensity. And Mr. Masefield's long poems are of the same kind.

The most famous of them, *The Everlasting Mercy*, is an example of this. It is an account of the conversion of Saul Kane, a village ne'er-do-well, ostensibly from a life of filth, greed, and anger, to a knowledge of Christ. But the sense of the poem is much more a turning of itself from a description of the external life of dissipation to a description of a consciousness of beauty within and without.

Doubtless this might be part of the greater conversion, but doubtless also it is not sufficient in itself to carry that high thing whose vastness and significance the mystics themselves have often laboured in vain to convey. In the first outbreak of abuse which occurs in the poem—

> 'You put.'
> 'You liar.'
> 'You closhy put.'
> 'You bloody liar.'

—the repetition, the expanded repetition, gives a sense of weakness; and so at the end the similes weaken, rather than intensify, what is meant to be a passion of abandonment to God.

> And in my heart the drink unpriced,
> The burning cataracts of Christ.

It is a fine line, but it *is* a fine line.

In the actual invocations of Christ, in the meditative prophecies of the new life that awaits the converted villager, this weakness is more suitable; for it is a proper part of their appeal.

> Lo, all my heart's field red and torn,
> And Thou wilt bring the young green corn,
> The young green corn divinely springing,
> The young green corn for ever singing;
> And when the field is fresh and fair,
> Thy blessed feet shall glitter there.

It is beautiful; it is the sigh of the romantic mystic, yet more the romantic than the mystic.

This is perhaps the reason why *Dauber* is more convincing, because the style and the central subject are more akin. *Dauber* is about art, and art—except in the greater artists—is a more partial, provincial, indulgent, and individual thing than religion. It is like the stone upon which man falls and is broken, whereas anything that can decently be called religion is like that which falls upon him and grinds him to powder. Dauber is an artist who goes to sea in order to

> '... know the sea and ships from A to Z
>
> . . . . .
>
> It's not been done, the sea, not yet been done,
> From the inside, by one who really knows.'

The poem narrates his persecution by the crew; his horrible experiences of Cape Horn and of the ice; his growth into a sense of the greater potentialities of art; his growth also into a fearless manhood; his death.

But because the efforts of man towards art are better subjects for discussion than mystical conversion, which is the most incommunicable of things, and because descriptions of the sea occupy much of the verse, the reader is not so conscious of a crisis

JOHN MASEFIELD

avoided as in *The Everlasting Mercy*. The last four stanzas are an example of the danger that haunts Mr. Masefield; they are at once too artistic and not artistic enough. They are a beautiful, quiet, detached ending to a story of turbulence and disaster.

> Then in the sunset's flush they went aloft,
> And unbent sails in that most lovely hour
> When the light gentles and the wind is soft,
> And beauty in the heart breaks like a flower.

This is a conventional ending, taking the reader away from those heaped seas and the falling body of Dauber; but the poem has not been conventional in that way throughout. The figures of the sailors should have been more formal and less semi-realistic if so formal an ending was to be borne. It is like a bit of mosaic work inlet into a violently representational wall-painting.

But the last line quoted above has given away one of Mr. Masefield's preoccupations, which is beauty. There can be few poets in whose verse the word occurs more often, though many in whom the thing itself occurs less often. More adventurous than many, Mr. Masefield has concluded his *Good Friday: A Play in Verse* with a small lyric by a Madman which ends

> Wisdom that lives in the pure skies,
> The untouched star, the spirit's eyes:
> O Beauty, touch me, make me wise.

It ought, one feels, to be more effective than it is. Can it be that *King Lear*, for example, might also be less tremendous if Albany had closed it with a short speech about the everlasting search for Beauty, or even *Macbeth* if Malcolm had referred to some sort of soft flowers that bloom in the spring? But what then—may not a poet have his gospel?

Alas, experience can only be countercharged with experience, not by a gospel, a meditation, or a dream. These plaintive melodies, appeals to some Platonic memory, are not sufficiently filled with passion to make them contrast, and perhaps transmute, the tragedies with which Mr. Masefield's Muse concerns itself. Sir Guyon may destroy the enchanted garden of Acrasia, but what has that faery to do with Antony's 'I am dying, Egypt, dying'? They are different modes of being; Mr. Masefield's finest poems are those in which he has for a moment united similar modes. An experience is communicated in some of his poems which is at once shadowy and romantic and yet sunlit and actual: as, for example, in a few poems which are almost after the style of the old ballads. Sometimes when Mr. Masefield is trying to be realistic he is capable of doing dreadful things. But in other verses, and chiefly where a certain fantasy is involved, he has made convincing work— the poem where Pompey's ghost comes riding to Caesar's house by night, or that where Saint Withiel flees from the hounds of hell, or that of the false O'Neill. This fantasy also is the cause of the success of the second part of *Reynard the Fox*. The first part of this poem, an account of the gathering of the hunt, is like a parody of an English meet, only Mr. Masefield's gravity forbids the idea. It is quite delightful to read

> The stables were alive with din
> From dawn until the time of meeting.

> A pad-groom gave a cloth a beating,
> Knocking the dust out with a stake.
>
> . . . . . .
>
> Len Stokes rode up on Peterkin;
> He owned the downs by Baydon Whin;
> And grazed some thousand sheep; the boy
> Grinned round at men with jolly joy
> At being alive and being there.

It is almost impossible not to do exactly the same at Mr. Masefield; especially when we know that also

> Joan Urch was there upon her cob,
> Tom Sparsholt on his lanky grey,
> John Restrop from Hope Goneway,
> And Vaughan, the big black handsome devil,
> Loose-lipped with song and wine and revel,
> All rosy from his morning tub.

The uncertainty whether John Restrop is the name of Mr. Sparsholt's 'lanky grey' or of one of the riders does but add to the general exuberance. Never have the names of houses, farms, and villages of an imagined English countryside sounded so real or fitted so slickly into rhyme before: even Mr. Minton-Price, (perhaps Colonel?) of the Afghan border, had the decency to come on a horse called Marauder; and Cothill, of the Sleins, chose his birthplace with a forethought to a chestnut mare with 'netted cords of veins'. It is all very English, very jolly, and sheer invention.

But in the second part we have the hunt from the fox's point of view, with even an attempt to suggest the fox's apprehension of the external world instead of our own.

> The windward smells came free from taint—
> They were rabbit, strongly, with lime-kiln, faint,
> A wild-duck, likely, at Sars Holt Pond,
> And sheep on the Sars Holt Down beyond.

It is not perfectly convincing: we are rather pretending to be the fox than being it. But it is through that fantasy that Mr. Masefield leads on to one of his simplest and most poignant effects—

> There was his earth at the great grey shoulder,
> Sunk in the ground, of a granite boulder.
> A dry, deep burrow with rocky roof,
> Proof against crowbars, terrier-proof,
> Life to the dying, rest for bones.
>
> . . . . . .
>
> The earth was stopped; it was filled with stones.
>
> . . . . .
>
> Then, for a moment, his courage failed,
> His eyes looked up as his body quailed,
> Then the coming of death, which all things dread,
> Made him run for the wood ahead.

It is the pathos of the hunted thing to which Mr. Masefield continually returns, and whenever his art manages to draw this subject into a real instead of a false simplicity it is that in which he excels. The hunt may be literal, as in *Reynard the Fox*, or metaphorical, as in some of his other poems where the hero is pursued by destiny. It is, however, exactly on this question of destiny that Mr. Masefield's touch is a little uncertain. He needs, for his full romantic pathos, a ruthless destiny, but then he needs, for his romantic Platonism, an ever-present Beauty too, and pathos and Platonism are ill bedfellows. The finality of tragedy and the finality of wisdom hardly go together; still less a sighing consciousness of tragedy and a wistful longing for beauty. The poet may have it which way he likes—either the phenomenal world means something or it doesn't; he may have it both ways, at separate times, but even the greatest poets can hardly have it both ways at the same time. Coincidences of that sort are coincidences rather of emotion than of passion, for there the intellect would have a part to play. When the great passions ride abroad there must be space and time between them; light or dark, the surrounding air must be emptied of one terrible presence before the advent of another fills it. But the emotions are companionable; they will walk and even chat together. Pathos and hope can easily make friends and be seen in the same tale or vision. And in one of Mr. Masefield's tales, or visions, they come very beautifully together. *King Cole* is one of his most characteristic poems. It has his realism, his proclaimed concern with the workers, his fantasy—King Cole's spirit permitted to wander earth 'helping distressful folk to their desire'; his pathos—the subject is a circus 'broken by bitter weather and the luck'; his feeling for animals; his wistful consciousness of beauty. King Cole meets the miserable circus company on their way to Wallingford, where they mean to play. But Royalty is there to lay a foundation-stone, and the disheartened Showman finds his caravans driven a mile beyond the town by official orders and a likelihood of playing to 'two children and a ploughboy'. Meanwhile, however, King Cole goes to the Prince and, partly by speech, partly by magical music, persuades him to bring the Court to see the circus. The performance is given, everybody is happy, and King Cole, after playing alone in the night, fades slowly away. It is, with the exception of King Cole's talk with the Prince, almost wholly a series of little pageants, each done in a few stanzas or less, and all different. There is the draggled circus at the beginning; there is a procession through the town; there are the children scattering flowers before Majesty; and the pageant of Majesty itself. But in the second of these Mr. Masefield has done what he has rarely done elsewhere; he has united his knowledge with his desire and transformed actuality with beauty.

> And round the tired horses came the Powers
> That stir men's spirits, waking or asleep,
> To thoughts like planets, and to acts like flowers,
> Out of the inner wisdom's beauty deep:
> These led the horses, and, as marshalled sheep
> Fronting a dog, in line, the people stared
> At those bright waggons led by the bright-haired.
>
> And, as they marched, the spirits sang, and all
> The horses crested to the tune and stept
> Like centaurs to a passionate festival
> With shining throats that mantling criniers swept
> And all the hearts of all the watchers leapt
> To see those horses passing and to hear
> That song that came like blessing to the ear.
>
> And, to the crowd the circus artists seemed
> Splendid, because the while that singing quired
> Each artist was the part that he had dreamed
> And glittered with the Power he desired,
> Women and men, no longer wet or tired
> From long despair, now shone like queens and kings,
> There they were crowned with their imaginings.

And with them, walking by the vans, there came
The wild things from the woodland and the mead,
The red stag, with his tender-stepping dame,
Branched, and high-tongued and ever taking heed.
Nose-wrinkling rabbits nibbling at the weed,
The hares that box by moonlight on the hill,
The bright trout's death, the otter from the mill.

. . . .

And over them flew birds of every kind,
Whose way, or song, or speed, or beauty brings
Delight and understanding to the mind;
The bright-eyed, feathery, thready-leggèd things.
There they, too, sang amid a rush of wings,
With sweet, clear cries and gleams from wing and crest,
Blue, scarlet, white, gold plume and speckled breast.

And all the vans seemed grown with living leaves
And living flowers, the best September knows,
Moist poppies scarlet from the Hilcote sheaves,
Green-fingered bine that runs the barley-rows,
Pale candylips, and those intense blue blows
That trail the porches in the autumn dusk,
Tempting the noiseless moth to tongue their musk.

The passage suffers from being extracted, because it does not come, as in the poem, as a contrast to the dull pain of mortality. But here if anywhere Mr. Masefield has united reality, with a small r, and Reality, with a capital. He has done something similar in *Right Royal*, the story of a horse-race, and a very good horse-race—with the jolliest metaphor from football that ever was.

As in football, when forwards heave all in a pack,
With their arms round each other and their heels heeling back,
And their bodies all straining, as they heave, and men fall,
And the halves hover hawklike to pounce on the ball,

And the runners poise ready, while the mass of hot men
Heaves and slips, like rough bullocks making play in a pen,
And the crowd sees the heaving, and is still, till it break,
So the riders endeavoured as they strained for the stake.

In these two poems, and in a few of his ballads, and a few of his lyrics (such as the famous *Cargoes*), Mr. Masefield has created his best crises. In some—*Cargoes*, and the ballad of Pompey (*The Rider at the Gate*)—he has been contented with the temporal crisis; in others he has sought to include a spiritual significance. But surely those pageants come from the dim romantic country where paynims and dreadful sorcerers and evil chances awaited the lonely rider, where in a magical world the wandering knight came under the stars to a doubtful hut amidst woods filled with the ambushes of Mahound, where pageants of months and seasons and virtues and sins moved through dreams of beauty and came statelily into the knowledge of the world through the arch that was Edmund Spenser.

End Piece

End Piece

Since the hunt broke from Eden
   at the end of the first day,
with hounds and high forms riding
   and the ever-taken prey,
who knows which destiny man betides—
the thing that runs or the thing that rides?

Man in his fury riding
   'twixt Hate and Cruelty,
man in his anguish running:
   what madness of soul know we,
that breaks the heart and blinds the sight—
the ache of the gallop or the flight?

Far over the downs and cities
   the dreadful hunting goes,
and men and beasts are taken
   by the teeth that end the throes;
but what wise prophet under the sun
knows if we ride or if we run?

Pity is somewhere passing,
   and somewhere Love goes by,
but the hunt broke forth from Eden
   under a darkened sky,
and over the earth the tumult pounds.
Who flies, who follows, the rushing hounds?

RALPH HODGSON

Mr. Hodgson's biography is a darker secret even than Mr. Masefield's. He is said to have been born about 1878; his *Last Blackbird* appeared in 1907, his *Poems* appeared in 1917. He is now Professor of English Literature at the Imperial University, Sendai, Japan.

It may be supposed that when Giotto drew his famous circle there was very little for the draughtsmen of the neighbourhood to say about it. There the circle was.

Much the same is the natural feeling about Mr. Hodgson's poems. There is, for purposes of poetry, one book—the *Poems*—of sixty-two pages of text. Of these pages, making allowances for individual taste, perhaps ten or twelve are not quite so good as the other fifty. Another ten or twelve are as good as anything else in English lyric verse. And there, in a manner of speaking, we are.

It is, certainly, a particular kind of English lyric, and it has been described by Mr. Hodgson himself much better than anybody else could do it.

> Reason has moons, but moons not hers
>   Lie mirrored on her sea,
> Confounding her astronomers,
>   But O! delighting me.

These are the moons of a particular world of poetry—the world which is governed by the moon, and all the associations of the word in romantic poetry, the interior moon. Reason—land and sea—reflects a life not its own. Land and sea, for the metaphor could not be carried on to include all that it should include without enlarging it. The moon, of which those mirrored moons are images, has shone on wild dwellers in the air and the forest, on that strange and all but Platonic menagerie which goes in a shining procession through English verse. The Albatross perhaps leads them—Coleridge's albatross would be at home over Mr. Hodgson's ocean—but Shelley's skylark and Keats's nightingale are there, and Blake's lamb and tiger, and Darley's unicorn. Even before those great romantics a poet of another age had—in his only verse of that kind—summoned as beautiful an animal—

> A milk-white hind, immortal and unchanged;

and Christopher Smart had called forth a mighty throng.

Mr. Hodgson has added another nightingale, who sings (like Patmore's—certainly the nightingale should be grateful to the poets) in Abyssinia, and a wren with it—

> The babble-wren and nightingale
> Sung in the Abyssinian vale
> That season of the year!—

and other beings too. Goldfinches (after which he names his own songs), 'a leopard bright as flame', 'a dotted serpent', 'the cinnamon bee',

> And everything that gleams or goes
> Lack-lustre in the sea.

But this bright and marvellous pageant meets another procession in his verse—the train of mortal animals, hurt or dying, the beasts on whom the sun and no unearthly moon pitilessly shines. The babble-wren and nightingale may be singing in Abyssinia, by Mount Abora; but some such 'singing-birds sweet' are also

> Sold in the shops
> For the people to eat,
> Sold in the shops of
> Stupidity Street.

Blake's tiger is near at hand, but so are the 'tamed and shabby tigers' of the creeping circuses of England.

The Bull to whom he gives a poem threatens the herd 'in the furnace of his look' (and the word seems strong enough here to describe Nebuchadnezzar's), but also he is a 'dupe of dream', old, abandoned, at the point of death. The 'loathly birds' that hover over him are direct neighbours of the 'goldfinches and other birds of joy' whom Mr. Hodgson's genius goes wonderfully snaring. Songs of innocence are interspersed with songs of experience. Fantasy and actuality go hand in hand, and both are real.

They are so real that here and there they almost act together. Which of them chose the adjective in that description of the serpent and Eve going

> Down the dark path to
> The Blasphemous Tree?

It is not given to every poet to find a new, appropriate, and surprising adjective for a noun which has been part of our common imaginative experience for centuries—new, at least, so far as our living poetry goes. But then the whole of that poem is a new presentation of the ancient myth; it is innocence—a rather childish innocence, certainly; not that of the Lady in *Comus*—becoming, most unhappily, experience. There are two poems on that subject: one—

Eve—in the terms of the old legend; one—*The Royal Mails*—a fable of Mr. Hodgson's own. In this a page is sent by a Prince 'of very famous fame' to carry letters to far-off cities, and allows himself to be deceived and robbed—like a score of others before him—by apparent merchants in the wood. It is his anguish which ends the prolonged lyric tale. The description of original happiness in both poems is exquisite—Eve

> Wading in bells and grass
> Up to her knees,

and the young boy starting

> down the hill,
> With Castle-bells and Fare-ye-wells
> And bugles sweet and shrill,

which become at the end

> Castle-bells and Fare-ye-wells
> And hornets in his ear.

Nearly all Mr. Hodgson's other poems are expressions of one or other of those states. They are either about Beautysprite or 'wretched blind pit ponies'; about the heartbreaking wonder of young love or the gipsy girl insulted by a loose-tongued man at a fair, about a soul stunned by 'the harmonious hymn of Being' or shocked by the stupidity of man. These things are not posed as philosophical opposites; they are loosed as poetic apprehensions. The infernal toast 'under the hill to-night' after Eve has eaten is no more and no less thrilling than 'the lyric might' of all creation in song.

The occasional phrases in which Mr. Hodgson

suggests a belief in reconciliation are not perhaps his most successful. They have not his own peculiar and piercing ecstasy. When his mind is on the ecstasy (as in the poem called *The Mystery*) it does not communicate the thrill as it does when he is gazing at some actual or imagined example of it. Moments of anguish, however, moments of delight so intense as to be nearly anguish, are on almost every page; the less convincing poems are very rare, and in a poet less perfect than Mr. Hodgson would not be mentioned. But when he does not so much argue as assert, we tend to become restive.

> God loves an idle rainbow
> As much as labouring seas...

Well, it's rather hard on the seas.

There is another miracle Mr. Hodgson has here and there worked, and that is the conquest of Time. One of his best-known poems is that which begins

> Time, you old Gipsy-Man,
> Will you not stay?

It is not in the least metaphysical; it has no relation to the Time in which Mr. de la Mare's poor Jim Jay got stuck. But it is extraordinarily effective; it really does communicate a sense of vast centuries in a few five- or six-syllabled lines. Another poem on Babylon is a protest against archaeologists and their excavations (here again we need not agree with the intellectual protest; after all, the Babylonians are not suffering as 'the wretched hunted hares' of *The Bells of Heaven* are). But the two chief things in it are an eight-line picture of Babylon at its height and a ten-line picture of Babylon in the desert.

> The soldier lad; the market wife;
> Madam buying fowls from her;
> Tip, the butcher's bandy cur;
> Workmen carting bricks and clay;
> Babel passing to and fro
> On the business of a day
> Gone three thousand years ago.

'But that', one's mind says, 'is not Babylon; no one ever talked of Madam and Tip in the city of Ashtoreth and such names. That is the life around us now. It is we who lived three thousand years'—and the verse has done its work. Within us is Babylon and contemporary London, and the whole airy curve of time that ends where it began. The period between is everything and nothing. And that is what one kind of poetry can do.

We come back to Giotto's circle. Mr. Hodgson's adeptness at it shows anyhow that, however much we may welcome the works of poets who do not care for rhyme and traditional rhythms, these things are still capable of producing new emotional wonders. The mere senses are more thrilled by Mr. Hodgson's verse than by that of any other modern poet. Even Mr. de la Mare, though he may enchant us more strangely, pierces us less deeply. The rhymes come so closely together—sometimes they have to be interior rhymes, so sharp, so immediate must the wound be.

> Castle-bells and Fare-ye-wells,
> And bugles sweet and shrill.

How ridiculous that that obvious conjunction was never made before! Even Tennyson's bugles are more faery and less piercing.

> When stately ships are twirled and spun
> Like whipping tops, and help there's none
> And mighty ships ten-thousand ton
> Go down like lumps of lead.

Dear rhyme!

And in that circle lie the seas of Reason and the moons that are not Reason's, and all those lovely beasts and birds, and the 'shy bat' that peeps at eve, and the 'prodigious bat' that comes from hell and is horrified to hear a goldfinch singing. And there too is innocence, and innocence lost, and singing birds 'sold in the shops for the people to eat', and others slain and despoiled by 'the pimp of Fashion', and cruelty to

> tamed and shabby tigers
> And dancing dogs and bears,
> And wretched blind pit ponies,
> And little hunted hares.

'O the pity of it! the pity of it, Iago!' For Beauty-sprite, unlike Desdemona, has been ruined indeed.

End Piece

End Piece

Innocence in the garden,
   innocence in the wild;
innocence taken,
   beaten, defiled.
     Ah it dies
through the heart's wound and the deadened eyes.

Innocence free and singing
   through all worlds weak or strong;
innocence moaning,
   bound with a harsh thong.
     Ah woe
that innocence must perish so!

Poetry went shining
   through a shining world;
round her the pipes
   of Asmodeus skirled.
     Ah see,
Poetry bleeds, dumb poetry!

WILFRID GIBSON

Born 1878. During the war he served in the ranks. His poems include: *Stonefolds*, 1907; *Daily Bread*, 1910; *Fires*, 1912; *Thoroughfares*, 1914; *Borderlands*, 1914; *Battle*, 1915; *Friends*, 1916; *Livelihood*, 1917; *Whin*, 1918; *Home*, 1920; *Neighbours*, 1920; *I Heard a Sailor*, 1925; *Collected Poems* (1905–25), 1926; *The Golden Room*, 1928.

Stonefolds, Daily Bread, Fires, Thoroughfares, Battle, Friends, Livelihood, Neighbours—these are some of the titles of Mr. Gibson's books. If he had wished to choose one of them for the title of his collected poems, perhaps *Livelihood* would have been the best. For the necessary seriousness which is attached to that word in most of our minds—in an age when money difficulties limit the freedom of nearly all our emotions—would stand for the greater part of Mr. Gibson's work; and yet a faint possibility of fantasy clings to it. Must not one of the lesser lyrists have used it somewhere? Are there not in one of our anthologies some such lines as

> The current of her pulsing blood
> through all her limbs I understood
> for my immortal livelihood?

Such a contrast of union is in Mr. Gibson's work and a critic might wonder which of his dispositions have produced the most lasting poems. It is a difficult question precisely because those longer and less lyric poems are difficult to appreciate properly. Take the opening of *The Machine*:

> Since Thursday he'd been working overtime,
> With only three short hours for food and sleep,
> When no sleep came because of the dull beat
> Of his fagged brain, and he could scarcely eat.

When a poem begins so it is clear that the reader will not have an easy task. No sudden dance of words, no dazzling flight of song, no felicity will come to his aid; if he is satisfied it will be by colloquial diction and conversational rhythm. Nor can he hope, as he will soon find, for any impetuous compulsion of the universe such as some poets provide. These poems are as likely to deal with quiet happiness as with drab misery, and with violent tragedy, or even with nothing at all but the passage of days, as much as with either. The mere simplicity of common words, holding the mere simplicity of common life, must do all the work. As the characters appear, in the dramatic pieces, or are described, in the narrative, we know that none of them will break into those torrential metaphysics which Mr. Abercrombie has never been able to refuse his cobblers or tramps or farm girls. If Mr. Gibson's people comment at all it is in such words as

> Daughter, it's strange how little happiness
> It takes to keep us going.

> Life's an old thimble-rigger, and, it seems,
> Can still get on the silly side of me,
> Can still bamboozle me with his hanky-panky.

> Life, the same job and the same jests over and over.

> Folk who stand on their rights
> Get little rest—they are on a quaking moss
> Without a foothold.

Life happening rather than Life desiring passionately to know itself is the subject here, and Life happening rather than the individual characters to whom and through whom it happens. Of the seventeen dramatic pieces which make up *Daily Bread*, one takes place on the highway, one in an engine-house, one in a slum-garret, eight in cottages in fishing or mining villages, six in 'a room in tenements'. It is the same kind of cruel and catastrophic existence which is shown everywhere. Everywhere these figures move along a narrow path between final poverty and immediate death, and, though they are differentiated from without for dramatic purposes, they have all grown from the same root. It may be that in his anxiety to differentiate them Mr. Gibson has spoiled his own aim. For the only criticism that could be offered (once accepting those conventions he asks us —and has every right to ask us—to accept in his poetry: that it should not sing or become passionately significant with music) is that they talk sometimes at rather too much length. In a long and extremely interesting piece, *Krindlesyke*, this is felt even more definitely. Bell Haggard is a magnificent creation, but she repeats herself; she likes to talk and be free and tramp the roads, and (merely because she tells us so too often) she almost outstays her welcome. The effect is to remind us not that Bell is this, but that Mr. Gibson is determined that she shall be. And therefore, all through these dramatic crises, we are conscious not so much of men and women as of Mr. Gibson presenting men and women.

But though perhaps these characters are not quite actual they have a relation to actuality. They are reminiscent of life; they convince us that thus and not otherwise in a million cottages and tenements men and women are behaving. We may not be moved directly by this tragedy of a fishing village, but we are so subdued that our hidden knowledge of the frequent real tragedy rises in our minds. And the movement does not stop there; this knowledge sends us on to the next poem and the next—apart from our own pleasure in reading—because here again, after so many poets have dealt with it, are man and his destiny, here is the life of man seemingly confronting the life of the world which is so much larger and yet (to our minds) so much less knowledgeable than man. It may defeat and destroy us, with its seas and droughts and shakings of the earth and machine accidents and all intellectual and spiritual distresses, but even in enduring them man seems to have something that it has not. Actually this may be all wrong; the sea may know when it destroys a fishing fleet and some kind of consciousness may inform a machine. But those possibilities do not enter into Mr. Gibson's verse, as they normally do not into our own appreciation of life. It is our knowledge against the world.

These figures then—life-size if hardly life-like, significant rather than symbolical, since symbols must have definite existence of their own—present to us the normal toiling life of man against a sky threatening storm and pierced by the gigantic chimneys of our modern industrial world. But though they signify many responses to circumstance, that which is common to them is, inevitably, endurance, accepted or imposed. And the quality common to much of that endurance is heroism. Heroes are hardly here, but heroic humanity is. *The Money* is one of Mr. Gibson's finest poems in this kind. It is about a woman who is found dead from starvation, wearing only 'a sorry rag', yet having in a silken bag 'tied with red ribbon round her neck' the sum of 'four-pound-seventeen-and-five'.

> 'It seems a strange and shameful thing
> That she should starve herself to death
> While she'd the means to keep alive.
> Why, such a sum would keep the breath
> Within her body till she'd found
> A livelihood, . . .
> But there was very little doubt
> She'd set her heart upon a grand
> And foolish funeral—for the pride
> Of poor folk, who can understand?—
> And so because she was too proud
> To meet death penniless, she died!'

This would be heroic enough. But this is not the secret. The poet, fantastically haunted by that ridiculous amount 'four-pound-seventeen-and-five', remembers how he heard the story of a miner burned to death in the pit. A 'deputy', remembering that he had been 'a neat and thrifty lad', rummages till he finds the money dropped from the dead man's pockets.

> 'And when it seemed there was no more
> I thought how, happy and alive,
> And recking nought that might befall,
> He too, for all that I could tell,
> Just where I stood had reckoned o'er
> That four-pound-seventeen-and-five.
>
> Ay, like enough—for soon I heard
> That in a week he'd looked to wed.
> He'd meant to give the girl that night
> The money to buy furniture.
> She came and watched till morning-light

Beside the body in the shed,
Then rose, and took without a word
The money he had left for her.'

. . . . . .

Then as I wandered through the rain
I seemed to stand in awe again
Beside that lonely garret-bed.
And it was good to think the dead
Had known the wealth she would not spend
To keep a little while alive—
His four-pound-seventeen-and-five—
Would buy her house-room in the end.

It is a perfect story, and it is paralleled by a true one. So, though not to such a tragic end, William Cobbett's betrothed lived a toilsome and painful life as a poor servant rather than spend any of the money he had given her. So hidden are the passionate motives of man.

The very next poem is of a small boy who carried his smaller sister home through a snowstorm. It might be sentimental, but it is not; it is heroic. What in lesser hands would be sentiment is here transformed —the easier perhaps for the mere childhood—into that virginity of spirit which is the condition of heroism. Heroism exists because the spirit is, in some way, sufficient to itself, untainted—in that one thing at least—by any desire beyond the perfection of its will. In a dramatic piece, *Summer Dawn*, a farm-labourer's wife encourages her exhausted husband to go out with her to earn a little extra money by hoeing turnips at three in the morning. While they talk he thinks of their courting days and says

Ah, those were happy times: we little thought....

She answers:

>You little thought? I knew—and still was happy.

'Had Mr. Gibson written often thus, it had been vain to blame, and useless to praise him.' Such compression of passion makes these low-toned colloquial lines as vital as great 'poetic' lines. In them, as in the dying speech of Cleopatra, the mind of man seizes on danger and hardship and overwhelms it.

Of the thirty poems which make up the section called *Battle* the peculiar characteristic seems to be the mingling of the ordinary life which has been abandoned with the violent and horrible life which has now become ordinary. Except for the statement of the facts there is no comment on that life; the poems are momentary incidents of destruction. But in most of them the knowledge of this incident is contrasted with the knowledge of normal things, and the unity of the two is in the mind which experiences them. Two may be quoted as examples.

Breakfast

We ate our breakfast lying on our backs
Because the shells were screeching overhead.
I bet a rasher to a loaf of bread
That Hull United would beat Halifax
When Jimmy Stainthorpe played full-back instead
Of Billy Bradford. Ginger raised his head
And cursed, and took the bet, and dropt back dead.
We ate our breakfast lying on our backs
Because the shells were screeching overhead.

His Father

I quite forgot to put the spigot in:
It's just come over me... And it is queer

> To think he'll not care if we lose or win,
> And yet be jumping-mad about that beer.
>
> I left it running full. He must have said
> A thing or two. I'd give my stripes to hear
> What he will say if I'm reported dead
> Before he gets me told about that beer!

The same is true of the section called *Casualties*, each of which is an epitaph or a brief lament. Each is headed by some name, but it is a question whether, artistically, they do not lose more than they gain by this. If the men thus remembered were actual individuals, piety has properly demanded what poetry might be more reluctant to give. Inevitably the names mean nothing to the reader; he is compelled to depend on the poem for his knowledge, and the poem would be more effective without this false aid—initials, or even (more austerely) numbers, would be a simpler and sufficient poignancy. Humanity, and not individuals, has always been Mr. Gibson's true subject.

But if the great mass of 'livelihood' forms the chief part of Mr. Gibson's work, there is still the fantasy, the little twist in thought or phrase that causes a new enjoyment for the reader. This is to be found in the longer poems, though it is more obvious in the shorter. In *The Crane* a boy of eighteen who cannot stand lies in bed, while his mother works, watching through the small window a gigantic crane, till he feels himself swung with it.

> My mother, hunching in her chair
> Day-long, and stitching trousers there
> At three-and-three the dozen pair,
> With quiet eyes and smooth brown hair...
>
> . . . . . .

> I wonder if 'twould bring her tears
> If she could know that I, her son—
> A man who never stood upright,
> But all the livelong day must lie
> And watch beyond the window-pane
> The swinging of the biggest crane—
> That I within its clutch last night
> Went whirling through the starry sky!

The Seal, in which a man dances with a seal who

> sheds her black and sheeny skin
> And smiled, all eager to begin;
> And I was dancing heel and toe
> With a young maiden white as snow
> Unto a crazy violin;

Flannan Isle—in which the lighthouse keepers disappear from an ill-fated island, leaving only

> a door ajar and an untouched meal
> And an overtoppled chair;

The Lodging-House, in which the poet climbs to his garret through a packed lodging-house, fearing when he reaches it

> Lest, when I fling it wide,
> With candle lit
> And reading in my only chair,
> I find myself already there,

and has to crawl back down the pit 'of Hell's own stair'; all these are examples of that fantasy which mingles with the ordinary human affairs of life.

Into these fantasies, however, the quality of heroism does not enter. In the extremer poems of this kind the incident is enough in itself, and the manner in which the mortal subject receives it is not dwelt on.

There is one poem (*Haunted*) of a man who is troubled by a perpetual nightmare of shipwreck and stabbing:

> Yet never in this life
> Have I used the butcher's knife,
> Never sailed the seas nor left my native shore;
> And I know not from what deep
> Stirs the doom that breaks my sleep
> To keep lykewake with the dead for evermore.

This, and others like it, are in some ways more directly effective, as poems, than the longer representations of man's slow and difficult life. For in them no effort is made to individualize the subject or teller of the incident beyond what expression the incident alone reveals. It is astonishing that a poet who has spent so much energy on presenting so many crises of our modern industrial life, who seemed to need a great pattern of iron and steel, or bare land and angry seas, for his background, should be able also to create such sudden poignant moments with no background at all, or rather with only the background that they themselves create. Perhaps the short *Wishing-Well* might serve as an example.

> Lass, I've heard tell
> That in this well
> The Roman folk would chuck,
> When things were going ill with them,
> A coin or so for luck.
>
> *And their great Wall's a ruin on the fell,*
> *And naught of their camp living but this well!*
>
> Ay, lass, that's so;
> And yet although
> Their rampart could not stand,

> Who knows but luck meant getting back
> Again to their own land?

> *So, you've chucked our last copper in the well?*
> *Well, what luck is or isn't, who can tell!*

But the question we always desire to put to a poet is how has he enlarged the experiences of English verse. Many poets are happily remembered for a few lyrics, some for one lyric alone. But man does not live his poetic life by lyrics, or when he does it is as much a brief emotional life as if he counted only the more extreme excitements of actuality. Even in a long poem it may well be that it is the lyrical moments to which we return most often, which we know and quote. But in a long poem they can exist more properly after their own being, they arise out of a more diffused manner of poetry and issue in it. It is therefore Mr. Gibson's ballads and lyrics and songs which we may read for thrills and for the crises of poetry, but it is the other kind of livelihood which we shall desire to live by.

It will probably take two or three more generations to decide Mr. Gibson's permanence in this kind. We ourselves are too aware of the thing about which he writes; we run too easily to read poems of our machine-controlled life. We can see the crowd pouring through the factory gates or round the mine-head, in the streets and the shops and the tenement-houses. We can hear their talk and their thoughts modulated into verse. But whether it has been modulated and enlarged into that expansion of experience which we call poetry is another matter. Yet the omens are good. Let one absurd omen be taken for fortunate—Mr. Gibson has been able to do something entirely fresh (after so many centuries!) with the moon.

> Night without a break
> Brooded overhead
> As we lay awake
> On our bracken-bed.
>
> So I shut my eyes,
> Burdened by the weight
> Of those starless skies
> And our luckless fate.
>
> But as I lay still
> She sat up in bed:
> *Turn your coppers, Bill—*
> *The new moon!* she said.

For the sake of Artemis and the strong heart of that luckless woman awake in the night, for the sake of the Immortals and the more heroic mortals, Mr. Gibson ought to be remembered in English verse.

End Piece

End Piece

Man goeth forth to his toil.
Between the harsh moor and the harsher sea,
harsher than either, grown to foil
his love, his longing and integrity,
the city rises; through the factory gate
pours in the human spate.

Man goeth forth to his toil:
little at evening to bring safely home
of leisure or of comfort, any spoil
from the laborious cornland or the foam
death-scattering, or the steel
hammer and bar and wheel.

Man goeth forth to his toil;
keeping beneath the everlasting doom
'mid griefs that rend him, angers that embroil,
on the cold highway, in a colder room,
for love or any wonder that may start
a patient welcoming heart.

LASCELLES ABERCROMBIE

Born 1881. He was Lecturer in Poetry at Liverpool University 1919–22, and has been Professor of English Literature at Leeds University since 1922.

His poems are: *Interludes and Poems*, 1908; *Emblems of Love*, 1912; *Deborah*, 1912; *Four Short Plays*, 1922; *Phoenix*, 1923; *Twelve Idyls*, 1928.

NEARLY all Mr. Abercrombie's published poetry is in a more or less dramatic form, sometimes capable, sometimes incapable, of presentation on a stage. But a drama of which the reader is perhaps even more conscious is the conflict between Mr. Abercrombie and his form. If that seem too insolent a criticism of one whom the authority of Alice Meynell called 'a major poet', let it be put another way; let us say that it is Mr. Abercrombie's mind which is dramatizing itself to itself and to his readers. In a sense, readers are more likely to say of those magnificent effects—'So that is how he sees it', rather than 'So that is how it is', and even then not to be quite clear how he really does see it. But this hesitation arises from the complexity of the poetry. It is not possible to read, for example, Hardy's verse without being quite clear how *he* sees it, and that quite soon; and a few fastidious minds have been repelled by what seems to them an over-simplification in the world that he sees. But then Hardy is a man of one idea, and that idea is a doctrine concerning the universe. Mr. Abercrombie's poetry, having many more ideas, has a very much more hidden doctrine—if indeed it has any. There are moments when the reader wonders whether there is any doctrine, as such, at all; whether the chief thing that this poet has done has not been to express for us merely life; a metaphysical, an intellectual, sense of life, no doubt, rather than a Shakespearian—but even Shakespeare is not our only poet. And the energy which pours itself through these poems is the energy of life itself, marvellously (as Mr. Abercrombie would say) considering its own nature, and attempting perfectly to know itself.

In such an effort, alas! the poetry of no single mind can succeed, and Mr. Abercrombie (whose critical books suggest a modesty too rare, even now, in criticism) would, no doubt, deny quite sincerely that he ever thought of succeeding, even that he ever thought of the attempt. But the attempt is there—not his, but his poetry's. The universal flow of things is making efforts to 'get itself said', to rise out of a tumultuous rush from moment to moment into a timeless lucidity. Hate and anger and love and lust and cruelty and pride and humility and delight and joy are engaged in trying to discover what indeed they are, and by that discovery to transmute and express themselves in a perfection of which they are only dimly conscious, if at all. Even Mr. Abercrombie's mind finds it difficult to control that primal strength of being; even there they find it difficult to achieve the end they desire.

At least it seems that this is something of what is happening, and it happens so rarely in modern verse that one would be grateful for it, even if the result were less superb than it is. Mr. Abercrombie referred once to 'a general process which is narrowing down man's methods of intoxication. Already we are practically limited to two forms, in which the intoxicant is still served without being timidly diluted—music and alcohol itself.' Either his modesty or his unconsciousness caused him to omit his own poetry, on which a man can get as drunk as need be—if he wants to. If—because, if not, he can occupy himself with asking, as the late J. S. Phillimore would have said, what this interesting and amazing noise is all about. For the noise *is* a dramatic noise; various people say things and do things, and though any one of them is liable at any moment to be whirled off his or her feet in the overwhelming rush of a metaphysical life, they make heroic efforts to stand up against the current, and at times very certainly succeed. But they succeed because Mr. Abercrombie's own mind is never intoxicated; he provides them with a footing and a stability which, merely in themselves, they would seem unlikely to retain. He keeps the ring; not quite fairly, because at times he is so entranced by the mere spectacle of this thought of life that he forgets his poor characters, and then the fight and the drama are over together, and nothing is left (in a double sense) but the shouting. And yet what a shouting! what language, what rhythm, what triumph!

It is one of the minor noticeable things about Mr. Abercrombie, almost alone among the older poets, and (for that matter) among the young ones, too, that he has not issued his Collected Poems. There has, of late years, been a great tendency among poets to issue some such volume after their first three or four books. It is an understandable but amusing tendency. This haste to be collected, this desire to be stabilized and permanent, attacks us all now in our poetic youth. What Shakespeare never did, nor Milton, we do now at thirty. But Mr. Abercrombie has not done it at forty odd. Some half-dozen volumes, of which the first two or three are out of print and only available to collectors, contain his scattered work. Of these, one is the longest and most significant—*Emblems of Love;* the rest may be grouped round it.

But this lack of a collected edition imposes on the reader a hesitation. Any poet, of course, may at any time issue a book which will make intellectual hay of everything that has gone before. Mr. Chesterton might become an atheist or Mr. Housman a Christian, and their poetry proclaim the fact. When, however, we have a *Collected Poems* before us we have a certain right to treat it as a whole, to submit ourselves to it as a single, if complex, experience, and consider our understanding of it. In this particular case we have no such right. More than with most modern poets, then, we must examine tentatively; not only may there be more to come, but the poet himself may be imagined to feel that his work is not yet finished; and even the decision and completeness of *Emblems of Love* may be modified by, or involved in, a farther reach of his mind. We have no assurance that Mr. Abercrombie's future will merely 'copy fair his past'; it is one of the things that make him exciting.

Emblems of Love was published in 1912. It has been followed by three volumes of plays—*Deborah* in 1922, *Four Short Plays* in 1922, and *Phoenix* in 1923. All these dramatic poems deal, if not with tragedy, at least with disaster; one or two of them indeed might almost have supplied Hardy with matter for a lyric or narrative study. *The End of the World* (in the *Four Plays* volume), for example, is an ironical presentation of a number of remote villagers overcome by the rumour and the conviction that the world is about to be struck by a comet. They are as fearful, as selfish, as distressed, as Hardy could have wished, and yet the effect is not in the least what his poem, had he written it, would have given. The reasons are obvious. The first is that, till we have read the poem, we do not in the least know what Mr. Abercrombie will make of it; we do not inevitably expect a particular doctrine, nor are we actually provided with any 'doctrine' as such at all. There are the people—they do and say certain things; but we do not know the end till the end, and the end is of poetic and not intellectual intensity. The second reason is that, as in Hardy not Dante himself (were he introduced) would ever be allowed to become exalted, so here any cobbler or publican may at any moment break into magnificent speech. It is, it must be allowed, Mr. Abercrombie's speech, not his own, but it is none the less thrilling; it may not be realistic drama, but it is, in a double sense, poetry. 'O think,' says the Dowser who brings the news,

> Life that has done such wonders with its thinking
> And never daunted in imagining;
> That has put on the sun and the shining night,
> The flowering of the earth and tides of the sea,
> And irresistible rage of fate itself,
> All these as garments for its spirit's journey—
> O now this life in the brute chance of things
> Murder'd, uselessly murder'd! And naught else

> For ever but senseless rounds of hurrying motion
> That cannot glory in itself.

So the Smith and the Wainwright talk—

> There'ld seem
> A part of me speaking about myself:
> 'You know, this is much more than being happy.
> 'Tis hunger of some power in you, that lives
> On your heart's welcome for all sorts of luck,
> But always looks beyond you for its meaning.'
>
> Why was I like a man sworn to a thing,
> Working to have my wains in every curve,
> Ay, every tenon, right as they should be?
> Not for myself, not even for those wains:
> But to keep in me living at its best
> The skill that must go forward and shape the world,
> Helping it on towards its masterpiece.

Even the unpleasant and pseudo-Puritanical Farmer says, casually, such things as—

> How should I not believe a thing
> That calls aloud on my mind and spirit, and they
> Answer to it like starving conquering soldiers
> Told to break out and loot?

Nor are such romantic similes the only ones; two lines above, the same character says—

> You watch me then
> Looking delighted, like a nobleman
> Who sees his horse winning an easy race.

The delight which the reader has in such similes and phrases, however, is nearly always felt only on the second reading; on the first one is too much concerned with finding out what is going to happen. Or even perhaps on a third; the first being for the story's sake, the second for the single complex poetic effect, the third for the details. The fourth might be for the intellectual assertions; the remainder for the mere renewal of delight. It is not every poet who will stand such repetition, but with Mr. Abercrombie they are not only desirable, they are almost necessary. Only a very steady poetic head (if there be such a thing) can take in at a first reading the mass of detail in every poem, and unless this is done the reader may do his author some injustice. Magnificence may seem to be merely magniloquence; the light on so many ordered swords of speech may seem to be merely a dazzling tumult;

> Like a great weather of wind and shining sun,
> When the airs pick up whole huge waves of sea,
> Crumble them in their grasp and high aloft
> Sow them glittering, a white watery dust,
> To company with light: so are we driven
> Onward and upward in a wind of beauty.

There are enough careful similes and intellectual exactitudes to save us from too drunken a result if we will observe their pauses; but they need that submissive observation.

The blank verse which has been Mr. Abercrombie's normal medium has itself helped to make a new freedom for English verse. During the Romantic Revival and the Victorian Age, the first efforts at breaking Milton's petrifaction of English blank verse began to succeed, but liberty was not fully won till our own time. In Wordsworth and Shelley the great things are, as it were, detached, and so also in Tennyson and Browning. They are not only separate from, they are even opposed to, the general effect; which is either colloquial or merely flat. Intentionally, as in Wordsworth or Browning, the blank verse became conversational; unintentionally, it became vapid in Shelley and dull in Tennyson. But by the work of many poets it has regained by now something of its late-Shakespearian ease; it can say colloquial things without being merely casual; it can rise or sink as it will; like Satan, moving through the chaos of unshaped thought, it

> With head, hands, wings, or feet pursues his way,
> And swims or sinks, or wades, or creeps, or flyes:

In that work Mr. Abercrombie has been one of the most industrious, and his own has entered into the freedom it has given. It can be matter-of-fact or rhetorical or meditative as it chooses; and it can do things with accents which perhaps only Milton dared. Indeed the lines are sometimes forced to an abruptness of division which Milton rarely allowed himself.

> Judith, we are two upright minds in this
> Herd of grovelling cowardice.

Lines like these, forced into each other, as it were, by the mere singleness of the meaning; lines of which fifteen or twenty go to one sentence, and this again is linked with such another; lines where an unexpected accent throws the reader violently forward into the next to recover the norm, or holds him up suddenly as if the verse broke away beneath him— all these go to increase that sense of something driving forward with an uncontrollable power, which creates in the reader's senses the same effect that the tumult of metaphysic creates in his thought—the effect of the urgent movement of the whole stream of being, desiring

> some high incomparable day
> Where perfectly delight may know itself.

The shorter dramatic poems are all presentations of some episode in this hurrying desire. *Emblems of Love* is the most complete statement of the theme and the most satisfying suggestion of the achievement. Its motto might very well be one of its own lines—

> That life hath highest gone which hath most joy:

and it is a study of that element in life which we call love—romantic love, sexual love—finding through the centuries and the generations its fullest capacities of joy. And more than a study, for it is an effort not only to tell us what love can do and be, not even only to show us love doing and being, but almost to be love doing and being. We know from Mr. Abercrombie's criticism that he will be content with poetry being little less than that, but it is an effort too great for any poet, and if there seems, to a tired mind, an occasional sense of strain in the poem it is because of this. Towards the end of the book, the similes, the lines and the phrases, the terms, God, Spirit, Being, leap upward in an attempt to soar as high as the great emotions they express. But even the exaltation of poetry cannot reach to that exalted and still delight of love transmuting itself into Deity, and it is with a wise skill that, in the most beautiful dialogue called *The Eternal Wedding* and in the *Epilogue*, Mr. Abercrombie subdues his imagination into a quietness and almost into fantasy—into a 'cool peace'.

Before this comes about, however, there are love's various strivings to be shown, from its beginning when the shaping imagination of man discovered that this great emotion was capable of being formed and, in turn, of forming him. The first 'scene' is in an encampment where two warriors of some ancient tribe are watching for an attack of wolves. One of them is still possessed by fear—of the stars, of the forces of the earth, and of women who are

> in league with the great Motherhood
> Who brings the seasons forth in the open world.

But the other has learnt another wisdom; in him has awoke the consciousness of the delight he takes in beholding women. A new glee is forming within him, a knowledge that beauty is beauty, the beginning of wonder, and

> Vision, that beats a timbrel in my blood.

The drama of the whole book is the crises through which this high possibility moves till it becomes at last what it can be. Through it

> Life is not life, but the desire of God
> Himself desiring and himself accepting . . .
> . . . God known in ecstasy of love
> Wedding himself to utterance of himself.

Between this beginning and this ending are five significant episodes; two traditional, and three invented. The women concerned in them are the Queen Vashti, three Scotch girls in 1745, and Judith who slew Holofernes. They stand respectively for prophecy of what is to be, for imperfect modes of love, and for the mystery of virginity. And in addition the goddess Ishtar in the first episode gives to Vashti, driven out of the palace by the offended pride of Ahasuerus, a vision of Helen, Sappho, and Theresa; of whom she says—

> Take none of these for perfect; they are moods
> Purifying my women to become
> My unexpressive, uttermost intent;

and perhaps the lines may be applied also to all the other women. There is no space here, nor would it be fair to Mr. Abercrombie, to attempt to describe those moods. This poetry demands close reading and close thought, and such poetry cannot be lightly—or indeed at all—re-expressed in prose. Arnold's claim that the loftiest function of poetry is the application of ideas to life, true as far as it goes, fails only to note that this application results in the creation of something with a new life of its own, and that the application of that life to ours is something profounder than the deduction of a moral or philosophical idea. It is the entering-in, through the senses and through the mind, of another existence. So much is true of the shortest and simplest lyric; much more of so highly complex a poem as *Emblems of Love*. Perhaps the most intense and most difficult episode is that of Judith, in which is set forth the presence of that virginity of soul

> impassion'd only
> To be as she herself would be, nor thence
> To loosen for the world's endeavouring.

But this virginity itself is that which Ishtar foretold,

> a perilous bridge
> Over the uncontrolled, demanding world.

It is after virginity has stood firm that the eternal wedding opens to those who have 'filled (their) soul with the need'.

> And every man and woman who has sworn
> That only joy can make this Being sacred
> Weaves at the wedding garment.

About this book Mr. Abercrombie's other poems may be gathered in a more or less direct relationship. All of them are concerned, one way or another, with man's imagination trying to shape the flow of things to its own desire. They are not like bits of a puzzle; they do not fit each exactly into its own place. They are, indeed, separate poems. But they leave the impression that they are all parts of the same universe (which, of course, they are), and that we have yet to find the rest of the stars which compose it. Whether we shall, depends on what Mr. Abercrombie allows us to see. There is no sort of repetition; one star certainly differs from another in glory, though their manner of speech has a certain semblance. *The End of the World* is a kind of fantasy on the End. *Deborah* is the tragedy of an attempt to shape life which fails. *Phoenix* is the shock of the actual world breaking in on a group of romantics—the 'world' here being represented by one of the most admirable 'wantons' (as the Elizabethans would have called her) in modern verse. *The Sale of St. Thomas* is an account of how the saint shrank from his mission to India, and how Christ compelled him by selling him to a sea-captain voyaging thither—denouncing his prudence

> For this refuseth faith in the unknown powers
> Within man's nature.

The dramatic poems in *Interludes and Poems* (1908) are still more metaphysical, and occupied largely with the thought of the meaning of Self; brooding over the nature of man and his needs—'desire of infinite things, desire of finite'. In the *Twelve Idyls* which form his latest book he has given us, among other things, a mythological poem on the sense of smell, based on the Book of Tobit, and he has reprinted *Mary and the Bramble*, an early poem, at once metaphysical and exquisitely sensitive. There runs through all of them, as through all this poet's work, that sense of life pulsing and striving to expand into its proper destiny, till

> thou shalt find thy knowledgeable desire
> Grow large as all the regions of thy soul,
> Whose firmament doth cover the whole of Being,
> And of created purpose reach the ends.

Any one who is not interested in those ends will probably not be interested in Mr. Abercrombie's work; the continual preoccupation with our mode of existence and its alternatives will tire him. Nor indeed, so far as the achievement of the poetry itself is concerned, is that the chief thing. But it is a very important element in the whole. For there is no other poet of our day who so occupies the inquiring intellect while astonishing the receptive, who so pleases the senses and delights the mind, or who offers his readers so many interesting states of being to explore and consider, or at times so high a sense of possible attainment. His own phrase describes Lascelles Abercrombie better than any other—

> All (his) speculation soareth up,
> A bird taking eternity for air. *End Piece*

End Piece

Infinite mountains of the interior mind
    cast their long shadow over field and town;
whence, from the melting glaciers far behind,
    comes the tumultuous torrent, rushing down
the deep-hewn watercourse of speech, and roars
    its meaning in its passage: our poor thought
feels how that sound old fruitfulness restores;
    flush with its banks philosophy is brought,
and metaphysic thunders once again
    over the pebbled channels of our time,
o'er rocky meditations to our plain
    of common hearing dashed, in rhythm and rhyme—
there, by the force of its creative will,
flows into poetry, surges, and is still.

T. S. ELIOT

Born in 1888, and an American by birth. His education is noteworthy for having proceeded not only at Harvard and Oxford, but also at the Sorbonne. He is the editor of *The New Criterion*. His books of poems are: *Prufrock* (1917), *Poems* (1920), *The Waste Land* (1922), *Poems 1909-25* (1926).

I

IN some former existence, among the myths of Greece, Mr. Eliot was probably a gadfly. Or perhaps, since no one knows either his own true shape or that of any other being or thing, perhaps he is now; and of that gadfly the Mr. Eliot who edits the *New Criterion*, that magazine of intellectual criticism, is but a spectre or emanation. But it is not the gadfly which drove Io across seas and lands, but rather one that stings us into a maze; a maze of which the divisions are only sometimes green hedges and are at others tombstones, and the walls of London drawing-rooms, and of mildewed cellars, and at others even whole landscapes. There is a clue to this maze, but we shall never know it, for the humming of the gadfly is unmeaning; though we have heard that its meaning is written in some very learned book which we shall never find, or sung by some dead poet whose lines we all but remember but never the needed, the significant, word. And after wandering in the maze for a long while we think that we have come out by the entrance and given up the search; only on some evening the talk veers to modern poets and we know we are not out—no, we are still there and lost and wandering, with thoughts full of those half-forgotten rhymes, always, always wandering, peevish and discontented and expectant.

In the maze, between the leaning tombstones or through the hedges, we catch glimpses of the strangest figures; we hear the strangest voices. Mr. Prufrock and Sweeney and Agamemnon and the figures on the Tarot cards and the Prince Ferdinand of Naples who was drowned and yet not drowned, and housemaids and rats, many rats. Bits of conversation float to us— 'I didn't mince my words, I said to her myself'; 'Cousin Harriet, here is the *Boston Evening Transcript*; 'You who were with me in the ships at Mylae'. Conversation in French, in German, in Italian. 'Are we then mad or is it poetry?' as a Victorian poet asked in effect of a similar welter of phenomena. It seems by no means clear.

This certainly is only an emotional response to Mr. Eliot's work. But—gracious goodness!—what else can one have? Have we the Upanishads and the Buddha's Fire Sermon and Miss Weston's *From Ritual to Romance* all to hand on our bookshelves? And yet the elucidation of one poem, *The Waste Land*, needs them, it seems, according to Mr. Eliot's notes. 'I recommend it [Miss Weston's book] to any who think such elucidation of the poem worth the trouble', the gadfly hums behind us. If only we could comfortably believe that it wasn't! If only we could neglect it, and go back to our sound traditional versifiers. They do not plague us with learned and inexplicable allusions. We know what they have to say, and that they have nothing to say is merely a proof of it. But then which of them, in their own line, has ever done anything half so good as

> The nightingales are singing near
> The Convent of the Sacred Heart,

And sang within the bloody wood
When Agamemnon cried aloud,
And let their liquid siftings fall
To stain the stiff dishonoured shroud.

Yet, beautiful as that is, for enrichment of the mind it is less valuable than a different kind of extract—
I have seen the moment of my greatness flicker,
And I have seen the eternal Footman hold my coat, and snicker,
And in short, I was afraid,

Since that most admirable phrase—'the eternal Footman'—occurs in the first poem in this book, and with the distinct knowledge that we have not the knowledge to find out Mr. Eliot's real meaning, it may be worth while to meditate on it. Whether the word 'eternal' here means 'timeless' or 'everlasting' doesn't much matter. Mr. Eliot is one of the few poets of whom one might hope that when he said eternal he meant eternal, and not merely immortal: in the first place, at all events, although the mind of man almost inevitably tends to ease itself by taking the first meaning to include the second. Certainly the consciousness of that Footman is felt in time; the word sums up a whole state of being. It is the experience, so common and so detestable, when the whole universe seems to be sniggering at one behind its hand, and at the same time obsequiously assisting the exhibition one is making of oneself. It is the transformation into a relation with things in general of that awful moment when, as regards things in particular, one feels that one is 'not quite'. It is the Dweller on the Threshold of the old traditions occupied on his modern business. It is Fear, blatant and ungentlemanly—especially ungentlemanly. Did one—*did* one forget to clean one's teeth?

In a sense, some of Mr. Eliot's poetry leaves the impression that to have teeth to clean at all, and to be under the necessity of cleaning them, puts an unfortunate man in a bad position with regard to the universe; much the same position the unfortunate wretch who forgot to clean them would be in with Mr. Kipling's Upper Fourth Remove. Only the universe is rather more caddish and snickers more like the Second Form than the Upper Fourth which would merely magnificently cut or kick. Actually Mr. Eliot brings in a tooth-brush at the end of one poem, called *Rhapsody on a Windy Night*. Rhapsody!

> 'The bed is open; the tooth-brush hangs on the wall,
> Put your shoes at the door, sleep, prepare for life.'
> The last twist of the knife.

It is a moonlit poem—but a modern moonlit poem, 'with all that those words connote'. It would be unfair to say that what those words do connote is merely Hell, but not very unfair. This is one of Mr. Eliot's simpler poems, and, whatever his more difficult poems mean, his simpler nearly always mean Hell pure and simple. But not in any prejudiced or invented mode. Mr. Eliot's poetic experience of life would seem to be Hell varied by intense poetry. It is also, largely, our experience. It is also, generally, our experience of Mr. Eliot's poetry.

But Hell, like heaven, has many mansions. If Mr. Eliot has gone to prepare a place for us, it is only courteous to attend, so far as we can, to the particular kind of place he has prepared: his eternal Footman ushering us, with the same snicker, through the door. The place was there before Mr. Eliot spoke of it; it may be that it is less there now that he has spoken of it. The recognition of his phrases is the recognition of our own experience, and the importation into that experience of some sense of enjoyment. Those mornings when we are

> aware of the damp souls of housemaids
> Sprouting despondently at area gates

(it is not the housemaids who are to blame; they are the jolliest individuals—it is the archetypal Housemaid who does so sprout) must in future be a little lightened by that phrase. And how entirely pleasant it will be to recognize at a particular moment in the afternoon that we also are turning

> Wearily, as one would turn to nod goodbye to Rochefoucauld,
> If the street were time and he at the end of the street.

Even the thought that we should know Rochefoucauld if we saw him—alas, the moment of our greatness flickers!

So with other phrases—

> My smile falls heavily among the bric-à-brac;

> The worlds revolve like ancient women
> Gathering fuel in vacant lots;

> I should have been a pair of ragged claws
> Scuttling across the floors of silent seas.

All these express in their different ways a common experience, a comment upon phenomena, a passive endurance of it, if nothing so violent as a repulsion from it. It seems as if Mr. Eliot reserved his strength for his intellect, especially for the expression of his intellect, and allowed himself otherwise to endure passively the tiresome assaults of the external world. By his mere passivity he infuses in those assaults a weakness. Against the hollowness of our own self-knowledge the hollowness of an immenser unknowing universe booms; on our own fantastic shadow-gestures obtrude yet more fantastic shadows, but shadows of no reality.

> This is the way the world ends
> This is the way the world ends
> This is the way the world ends
> Not with a bang but a whimper.

In the widespread revolt against taking ourselves tragically which has affected our minds, the contradiction of the grand style, and the magniloquent rant, and the flaming gesture which are so dear to the second-rate mind, Mr. Eliot's influence must have been one of the most effective: though it would be a bold critic who would venture to say that this was in the poet's intention. God only knows what was in Mr. Eliot's intention. But compare with the tragic solemnity (and general untruthfulness nowadays, whatever may have been the fact in the eighteenth century) of Goldsmith's famous quatrain this variation of it, which occurs in Part III of *The Waste Land*.

> When lovely woman stoops to folly, and
> Paces about her room again, alone,
> She smooths her hair with automatic hand,
> And puts a record on the gramophone.

The relief of it! the pleasure with which we hear

Oliver rebuked, or at least passed by; Mr. Eliot would not stop to rebuke him. How much more satisfactory, to us who live in it, is the recognition of the way things happen in this almost automatic hell, than any attempt to impose morality on it and to wring significance from it. The difficulty with moralists is that their readers are never sure whether they are not forcing the world into a code on the chance of it saying something intelligible; and then declaring that the noises it makes in that Scavenger's Daughter of law are full of the highest significance. If there is significance here it at least arises from a just recognition of the facts—'unreproved if undesired.'

But this reminiscence of Goldsmith brings us to another matter. Reminiscence (which fools call plagiarism, and annotators used to point out drearily and with none of the excitement of delight it should convey) is 'a law, not a privilege', of Mr. Eliot's verse. Reminiscence, and even direct quotation, sometimes recognizable, sometimes (by less learned minds) unrecognizable. We do not all know our Webster and Middleton as he does.

>   Here, said she,
> Is your card, the drowned Phoenician sailor,
> (Those are pearls that were his eyes. Look!)

That at least is Shakespeare and familiar. But—

>   'What is that noise?'
>   The wind under the door.

This is a reference to Webster, it seems,—'Is the wind in that door still?' Very few of us would have known it.

But this is not only a symptom of Mr. Eliot's manner of thought; it is a sign of what may turn out to be a growing tendency on the part of English verse. So rich now is our inheritance of associations in literature that it is beginning to be difficult to avoid them in creating new. Mr. Eliot has not only refused to avoid them; he has deliberately made them a part of his own language. We approach a form of poetic life which acts through the earlier myths of verse. Helen, Faustus, Romeo, Arthur, Abdiel—these have been allowed us in the past. But less familiar names have been (naturally) less used. Mirabell and Millamant, the White Devil, these have been left to criticism. They are now becoming new modes of expression. This new development, if it proceeds, will make poetry a more specialized thing; for the specialist it will become more exciting and intriguing. Poems will be composed wholly of remote and echoing phrases from the lesser-known medieval Spanish poets. The astonishing thing is that they will at the same time be new and beautiful poems. But our knowledge of our contemporary poet will arise from the method with which he deals with those phrases, from his evocation and control of them. We shall see him in a glass, but not at all darkly, perhaps more clearly than if he had composed every line himself.

To this extreme apparently Mr. Eliot has not gone; quite a large number of his lines are his own creation. His method varies between direct creation and evolution; fundamentalism and modern science agree in his verse. He is a union of opposites and yet a true union. It has been said that Mr. Housman wonderfully unites in one poem a common flatness and an uncommon beauty. But Mr. Eliot rather unites an uncommon flatness and a common beauty. For the flatness of these poems is always a particular and chosen flatness, and the beauty, though it may also be in a particular and chosen quotation, is at the same time a general echo of our literature rather than a particular new descriptive effect. Two quotations may show this. The first is from the end of Part II of *The Waste Land*.

Goonight Bill. Goonight Lou. Goonight May.
                      Goonight.
Ta ta. Goonight. Goonight.
Good night, ladies, good night, sweet ladies, good night, good night.

Many of his readers must so have felt sounding within them the young freshness of lyric as they heard goodnights exchanged outside a public-house, so near are we to both. Again:

> A rat crept softly through the vegetation
> Dragging its slimy belly on the bank
> While I was fishing in the dull canal
> On a winter evening round behind the gashouse
> Musing upon the king my brother's wreck
> And on the king my father's death before him.

Royalty is fallen to the rats here—in more than one sense; but the royalty is rich behind the rats. In those unforgettable lines we cannot see majesty except in decay, and yet in that decay the majesty that was appears.

But these perhaps are the *refrigeria* of Mr. Eliot's hell. We refresh ourselves in them, but they do not stop with us. Even the eternal Footman passes. For while he was imagined, the universe was given form and separateness, and there was always a possibility that we might either become used to him or feel a strong dislike of him. The use to which it seems we must finally become accustomed is quite as human an emotion, but less personally directed, In *The Hollow Men* there is a most admirable quatrain which contains more sense of mere hollowness than anything else Mr. Eliot has written. Even the quatrain quoted earlier on 'This is the way the world ends' introduces a bang, if only to reject it. But in this other stanza a traditional poem is varied by a few words, and an entire cold futility absorbs everything. Futile, imbecile, gyratory, we perform our antics— Mr. Eliot and his readers among us:

> Here we go round the prickly pear
> Prickly pear prickly pear
> Here we go round the prickly pear
> At five o'clock in the morning.

Hell; certainly hell. But then who ever really doubted it?

II

'Hence the soul cannot be possessed of the divine union until it has divested itself of the love of created things.' The quotation, from St. John of the Cross, precedes a *Fragment of a Prologue* which Mr. Eliot published in the *New Criterion* (October 1926; January 1927). On the title-page of his *For Lancelot Andrewes* (1928) is set a prayer: 'Thou, Lord, Who walkest in the midst of the golden candlesticks, remove not, we pray Thee, our candlestick out of its place; but set in order the things which are wanting among us, and strengthen those which remain, and are ready to die.'

In an age plagued by facile and therefore false mysticisms the full harshness of that first extract is apt to be overlooked. Mr. Eliot has himself deprecated the finding of cosmic significances in his work. But prayer and the meditations of the mystic must have no very different suggestion as signs to poetry than as signs to the acted poetry which we call living. Under the light of such words, the fantastic poignancy of the creatures of that *Agon*, prostitutes and their clients, remains piercing but becomes perhaps more terrible. Their insane songs, their heavy politenesses, their anxious credulity, the whole collapse is still a thin wail, but the echo of it is different. It turns us back to the first page of Mr. Eliot's *Collected Poems*, where the *Love Song of J. Alfred Prufrock* was preluded by a quotation from Dante. Dante and St. John of the Cross—what interpreters of poetry are these? Can this hell be rather the place of purgation? and has the eternal Footman himself some likeness to the Ancient of Days?

Mr. Eliot is right certainly to warn us against searching for—what our fathers desired so much— a 'message'; we shall not write little books on 'T. S. Eliot and how he has helped me'. But it does, nevertheless, with or without the poet's consent, direct towards some idea the associated intellect, and that idea here seems to be of some place of change— perhaps where corruption puts on incorruption.

End Piece

End Piece

Put out the light and then put out the light,
   quietly the faithful mind puts everything out,
   not with a gesture, not with defiance to flout
the lamps (the ranter called them) of heaven, nor spite,
but waits till the theatre empties; then with the flight
   of our tangled spectres, after the last tired shout
   of applause, time ends. The attendants will go about
the empty corridors, putting out even the night.

Emptiness and fullness wholly alike enjoyed,
since enjoyment must be, even of bleakness and void;
   mingled extremes and delights of poetry—
attentive in both, a mind hath everywhere stirred
to (O hark, hark! all richness held in a word)
   to entertain divine Zenocrate.

EDITH SITWELL, OSBERT SITWELL, SACHEVERELL SITWELL

Sir George Reresby Sitwell, himself an author, is their father. For details in their own careful phrases reference must be had to *Who's Who*. Miss Sitwell edited *Wheels: an Annual Anthology of Modern Verse*, in 1916; among her own books are, *Clown's Houses*, 1918; *The Wooden Pegasus*, 1920; *Bucolic Comedies*, 1923; *The Sleeping Beauty*, 1924; *Troy Park*, 1925; and *Gold Coast Customs*, 1929.

Osbert Sitwell published, among others, *Argonaut and Juggernaut*, 1919; *Out of the Flame*, 1923; *England Reclaimed*, 1927; volumes of travel, short stories, and a novel.

Sacheverell Sitwell: *The People's Palace*, 1918; *The Hundred and One Harlequins*, 1922; *The Thirteenth Caesar*, 1924; *The Cyder Feast*, 1927.

THERE was once a man who made a hobby of pursuing and collecting false dichotomies, which in practice he found to include pretty well every dichotomy. It is said that on his death-bed he was haunted by the question whether his very pursuit of them had not in itself created and nourished a false dichotomy of the finest kind. However that may be, one of his subjects which he found most prevalent was the distinction between literature and life. This appeared almost everywhere, in histories of literature, works of criticism, popular literary periodicals, and the daily papers. It was even to be discovered, concealed but present, in the works of most modern poets. In fact, it is reported that he eventually declared the only places which were entirely free from the pest to be the poems of Miss Sitwell.

In what way then does Miss Sitwell differ from her contemporaries that she has been able to avoid this division? and how is that division to be discovered in their poems? It is of course obvious that when they are producing their finest work this division between literature and life does not arise. There is then present in their lines that energy which creates new things, and (for all we can tell) does not much mind whether it is a baby, a scientific formula, or a poem. The product is a living thing to our apprehension: it communicates that sense of existing in its own right which we all recognize that the greatest achievements of verse possess. The writer rather discovers than makes it. It is; it is literature but it is also life, it is life although we call it literature. But when this energy departs, and the poet is left to put in a little 'putty' (to use an admirable word of Mr. Robert Graves, who has asserted that there is no poem in existence without some putty, however little)—when this happens, we find them writing *about* the world. We can even agree or disagree; we ask whether the cuckoo is heard in October or the philosophy can be justified by reason, or the characters are behaving consistently, and other interesting questions. A good deal of criticism is concerned with them, but unless such criticism is merely an approach to the moments of energy, it is a game—a very enjoyable game, but a game. At the moment when this possibility of agreement enters in, the regrettable dichotomy appears. The poem has become something other than triumphantly creative energy; it is writing about life. It is, at its best, literature. It is, at its worst, literary. There are other depths, but they may be ignored.

It would be absurd to pretend that Miss Sitwell, in her poems, never loses this fullness of energy. But her distinction is that, when she loses it, she does not begin to write about the world. Her putty is bought at her own shop and not at a common store. Her world may be a small world, even (to some tastes) a displeasing world, but it is at least a world. It is very rarely possible to agree or disagree; it is quite possible not to understand, but that is largely because we are not yet there. Mild and magnificent eyes we are used to, and to the slight haze that comes over them as the clear accents begin to harden a little. But Miss Sitwell's eyes are another matter altogether.

Not that even Miss Sitwell, in the prose fragments she prefixes to certain of her groups of poems, does not occasionally allow life to creep in as a thing separate from literature. 'This modern world is but a thin match-board flooring spread over a shallow hell. For Dante's hell has faded, is dead. Hell is no vastness—' and so on. But what persistent dichotomy is this? why must we formulate to ourselves a disappearance we are perfectly willing to accept instinctively while we read Miss Sitwell? Why must we consciously abolish one meaning of Hell before we can accept it as

> just as properly proper
> As Greenwich or as Bath or Joppa?

Must we deliberately turn Farinata out of his tomb in order to see

> the peruked sea whose swell
> Breaks on the flowerless rocks of Hell?

We should have forgotten him for long enough if Miss Sitwell had not dichotomized.

But, forgetting him again, let us enjoy the new world—hell and all. And this enjoyment raises a question which perhaps does not, in its answer, cause the division it seems to imply. Is this world a world of two dimensions or three? To emphasize, as has sometimes been done, the eighteenth-century nature of it is merely a concession to laziness. Miss Sitwell's world is no more eighteenth-century than twentieth or twenty-second or whatever period it was in which

> Said Il Magnifico
> Pulling a fico—
> With a stoccado
> And a gambado
> Making a wry
> Face: 'This corraceous
> Round orchidaceous
> Laceous porraceous
> Fruit is a lie!
> It is my friend King Pharaoh's head
> That nodding blew out of the Pyramid. . . .'

(Did Mr. Polly also write poetry?)

But sedan chairs do not make an eighteenth-century, nor are those charming fairies who come in them, and 'descend from each dark palanquin', carried from any Augustan age. The eighteenth was the most mannered century of which most of us have heard, but that is not a sufficient reason for accentuating the colours and shapes Miss Sitwell has found in it. It is the whole world, and not one period, which she draws up before us; draws up from where it lies 'deep-meadowed, happy, fair with orchard lawns', and hangs it right up like a two-dimensional, yet opaque, curtain, with all those colours and shapes and sounds and feelings changing places and slipping one into the other, so that (in what is becoming her most notorious poem—*Aubade*) 'The morning light creaks down again'. (Miss Sitwell has defended the phrase and said it does; alas! *Is* the cuckoo heard in October?) Or

> By white wool houses thick with sleep
> Wherein pig-snouted small winds creep,
>
> With our white muslin faces clean,
> We slip to see what can be seen.

Or

> Astronomical
> Trees where swoons
> The breeze, hide coxcomical
> Lanthorn moons
> Set in the trees
> Like bird-lime.

This unusual and quivering curtain is of sound even more than of colour and shape. To say that poems are musical is sufficiently depressing praise, but Miss Sitwell's are musical with a difference. They seem to be becoming music; they dance in a Protean changing between sense and sound, now one, now both, now—but they never become *that*. There is a poem called *Fox Trot* which is a pure joy:

> Old
>   Sir
>   Faulk,
>   Tall as a stork,
> Before the honeyed fruits of dawn were ripe, would walk
> And stalk with a gun
> The reynard-coloured sun
> Among the pheasant-feathered corn the unicorn has torn,
>   forlorn the
> Smock-faced sheep

> Sit
>   And
>   Sleep,
> Periwigged as William and Mary, weep...

Words and fox-trot movement; here are the two dimensions. Who can insist on having depth, and (for all one knows) meaning?

It is this extraordinary arrangement of sound which must have captured the first shy and eager attention of many of Miss Sitwell's readers. This, and direct fun. It *is* delightful to think of Queen Victoria in *Hornpipe*:

> Queen Victoria sitting shocked upon the rocking-horse
> Of a wave said to the Laureate, 'This minx of course
> Is as sharp as any lynx and blacker-deeper than the drinks and
>   quite as
> Hot as any hottentot, without remorse!
>   For the minx,'
>   Said she,
>   'And the drinks,
>   You can see,
> Are hot as any hottentot and not the goods for me!'

The force with which Victoria speaks is a real tribute to a myth which deserves at least a respectful mockery. The large flat surface before us opens in such poems into perspectives of suggestive sound. It is almost as if we were gazing at the taut cover of a large drum, painted with curiously intertwined figures, while Miss Sitwell, playing on the other end, drove waves of varying music towards us.

But a drum is a crude metaphor, and will only serve for those poems where her fun is at its broadest. If the drum begins, other instruments take up the sound, and any one entering on those corridors of music may find this two-dimensional world taking on a three-dimensional life. But it is still that world and not another, not the ordinary world of life. Even in those moments when the reader begins happily to wonder whether Miss Sitwell has not only a human but actually a womanly heart, it is still Miss Sitwell of whom he is wondering. It is from her own particular and convinced imagination that such a fantasy as this arises:

> at the hot sand's edge
> Anchored by waters like the sound of flutes
> Our nurses sat; it seemed, I thought, they listened.
> And they were black with shade, and so we named
> Them Asia, Africa, and still they seem
> Each like a continent with flowers and fruits
> Unknown to us...

This beauty is in no sense alien to the other strangenesses, but the strangeness and beauty are one. Every good poet, universal at his best, is individual in his second degree, characteristic at his third, and for the rest merely, even if interestingly, commonplace. Miss Sitwell, it must be admitted, is hardly ever commonplace; whether she is instead something worse or better at times is another question. *Hardly* ever; she falls occasionally to the word 'dream' or 'loveliness for ever young'. In the exquisite *Troy Park* are the lines:

> And shall we never find those diamonds bright
> That were the fawn-queen of Palmyra's eyes?
> Ah, dark hot jewels lie hidden from the sight
> Under dark palm trees where the river sighs
> Beyond the tomb of young eternities.

'What', as my lord Macaulay might have observed, 'a young eternity may be, what its tomb may be, what the river that sighs by it may be, and what kind of dark hot jewels lie hidden from sight under the dark palm trees where the river sighs' are questions (it is only fair to Miss Sitwell to change to a loftier writer) 'above Antiquarism. Not to be resolved by Men nor easily perhaps by Spirits, except we consult the Provincial Guardians or Tutelary Observators.'

But it is not the 'young eternities', nor even their tombs, that make up the distances of Miss Sitwell's imagination. The perspectives of music become perspectives also of time and sadness. Now opening into a lovely depth, now closing up into a brilliant superficies, the poems of *Troy Park* and *The Sleeping Beauty* are all an evocation of, and a lament over, *le temps jadis*. Childhood and age spread out; 'the child who saw Midas' and the old Duchess of Troy. It must be deliberately that the great name of Troy is used in these poems for that high fantastic country house where 'Dagobert and Peregrine and I' wander as children or

> On the grey and mondaine grass of Troy Park
> The Countess's two dogs run and bark
>
> While the long glass stalactites of the rain
> In the endless avenues sound again;

and the ghost of King James appears at the window, and the lady's maid folds up the dresses, and again and again the landscape changes into that romantic China our childhood knew in pictures (another tradition of conventionality, as much as the eighteenth century), so that we cannot tell whether those figures in crinolines or pelisses are walking with mandarins

over small fantastic Chinese bridges or by the autumn
moats of English parks, and a rain of desolation falls
softly out of some existence over some non-existence,
and everything is faint and small and heart-break-
ing, and African music breaks in a storm of laughter
through it all.

But among these is a sense of growth in knowledge;
of spiritual adventure, were it not that all adventure
seems to resolve itself into spiritual endurance. This
is perhaps most to be felt in *The Sleeping Beauty*.
For this poem contains, in Miss Sitwell's degree,
that sense of change and the passing over from one
state of being to another which is to be discovered
in the work of nearly all poets of whose work more
than a lyric or two has survived. In a poem which
produced more sense of thought, and less sense of
sound and sight, and those sounds and sights them-
selves melodies and arabesques of romantic know-
ledge, the story would be symbolical. It is at least
a symbolism of emotion, but the emotions are so
intermingled that it is difficult to be sure what central
one most affects the reader. Here is Mrs. Troy, who
is as like the Mrs. Southern of Osbert Sitwell's
England Reclaimed as the Dagobert of *Troy Park* is
like himself; and here the fairies of Perrault; and
a Soldan singing of swarms of gold that will 'fly like
honey-bees'; and Jane, who this time is not awakened
by the creaking morning light but 'forgets the time
... in sleep's dark grove'; and the Dowager-Queen,
'so frail with age she cannot wake'; and Malinn the
housekeeper's daughter, whose

> reynard-coloured hair
> Amid the world grown sere

> Still seemed the Javanese sunrise
> Whose wandering music will surprise
> Into cold bird-chattering cries
> The Emperor of China
> Lying on his bier.

Those lines are part of this individual beauty. There is perhaps the smallest suggestion that it is an esoteric experience of which we are reading instead of being one common to man; there is an occasional line where Miss Sitwell writes more like, let us say Mr. Yeats, than is usual with her, as when she speaks of 'songs no heart can understand'. But it is a beautiful and exquisite thing, full of thrilling images; and childhood and death are continually moving through it, between the 'dark palanquins' of the fays.

If the eighteenth century from time to time appears in Miss Sitwell's poems, the manners, the retired self-consciousness, it is an earlier period that her brother Sacheverell recalls. He has been compared to the Elizabethans often, and necessarily, enough; the richness and freshness of some of his lyrics are a complete justification. But the difference is there too—he is their antitype in manner. For most of the Elizabethan songs, however complicated, are simple enough in sense; they riddle gaily. It was not till nearer the Carolines that the shadow of the intellect fell on the lyric and its strength began to enter. Mr. Sitwell's lyrics are rich and beautiful, but not gay. Nor is it only the intellect that makes them difficult. They are aromatic gums, but hardly flowers.

His 'Variations' on a theme by George Peele are an example of this; there are three of them, growing in complexity. But the sound of the opening of the first, though in a shorter metre, is longer and weightier than its original.

> God, in the whizzing of a pleasant wind,
> Shall march upon the tops of mulberry trees.

So Peele; and Mr. Sitwell—

> I was lying in the dappled shade,
> the lute hung lifeless in my lap,
> When God stepped out of a moving cloud
> to tread the tops of mulberry trees.

It is perhaps over scrupulous to see in the difference between marching and treading the difference between the two poets, although Mr. Sitwell's longer rhythms do seem to tread rather than to march, dance, or 'move high and disposedly'. They are sometimes heavy with their weight of riches; their embroidery of unicorns (the unicorn pursues these poets so determinedly that he will gallop himself out of English verse for awhile) and waters and flowers.

> The walking of the [poems] across the bridges, down the alleys,
> has not the march of soldiers, or the feet of dancers,
> but is the roll of waters, the balanced tread of sailors,
> who cross the shaking hills of sea under every wind and sky.

'Men', Mr. Sitwell wrote, but it is not merely fantastic to see his poems also as crossing 'shaking hills' of shifting visible phenomena and changing philosophic values—'where the cruel lights whine' or 'yellow is wrong for the corn's dark yield'. His world is larger than his sister's, but less entrancing. Larger, for it deals much more often and definitely with the present external world; it has a greater medley of things, natural, and fabulous, and of great art. But larger also because it is striving with philosophy, and asking intellectual questions.

What is sin? Where does virtue lie?
Is yellow wrong for the corn's dark yield or green for rye?

The phrase is as illuminating as it is dexterous, but it is a little too dexterous. Yet it is a phrase of the imagination, only its intellect has quenched emotion. Donne erred so sometimes, and in one poem (a canto of which is included in each of three separate books, and a fourth promised) Mr. Sitwell has taken Donne as one of his heroes, the others being Gargantua, and a third—whom the reader at first imagines to be Mr. Sitwell but afterwards discovers to be, apparently, God. This whole poem, *Dr. Donne and Gargantua*, is an immense 'variation' on two lines of Donne's

> Run and catch a falling star,
> Get with child a mandrake root.

This is what the two set out to do—a magnificent adventure!

> Gargantua said he would contrive
> to get a mandrake root with child.
> Doctor Donne had said he'd strive
> to snare a meteor, wet and wild.
> And so they set out from the Alps
> which showed more white than old men's scalps.

It is a comment on the dullness with which we normally read poetry that no young worker has thought of taking Donne's lines as a subject before. How much more royally dangerous and fantastic than 'the life Of Arthur or Jerusalem's fall'—and yet Coleridge thought the last the only epic subject that remained! The Grail quest itself dwindles in comparison.

To analyse the poem, however, would be to undertake an almost equally arduous adventure and one for which there is here no space. It seems an attempted summary of all the quests of humanity, treated half-philosophically, half-satirically. But what is the end is hidden in the unpublished fourth canto.

There is in it, in spite of the lovely lines and the agile intellectual comedy, something that, a little, drags. But it is probable that this is due, not so much to any lack in Mr. Sitwell's capacities as to a general difficulty of our time. In this harsh age our self-consciousness has passed into our poetry, and lies upon it with a weight 'heavy as frost and deep almost as life'. This frost may itself be covered with richness, as if our poets held a harvest festival at Christmas, but except for a few lyrics it holds the land prisoned. Yet how lovely the richness and the lyrics can be any one need only open any of Mr. Sitwell's books to see. The short poems under the general title *Hortus Conclusus*, which are to be published in a book by themselves, are—of all his poems—most like flowers; as *White Hyacinth* and *Kingcups* may show.

Kingcups

When poetry walked the live, spring wood,
Hid, ghostlike, in the leaves' green hood
She came to a slant fence of sun,
Whose golden timbers, one by one,
Trod into a marsh's toils
And here she stayed her flowery spoils;

> But pitying the marshes' plight
> She shook her lap, and wide and bright
> Great kingcups to that waste she threw
> Where nothing lived, and nothing grew;
> Now, where poetry passed, there stays
> The light of suns, the fire of days,
> And these cups for kings to hold
> Make summer with their wide-eyed gold.

White Hyacinth

> For flower of day's pale light, I'll say
> The hyacinth, sweet foot of day,
> Still smelling of the star's wet wood
> In midday's high and lonely mood;
> The gales from that Hesperides
> This keeps and stores up for the bees,
> Who little know while at their honey,
> This liquid gold is alien money.
>
> Yet, while they eat, the taste is strange
> And drowsiest of their wingèd range;
> For hyacinth never sleeps, the dew
> Fast drying, as the stars get few,
> Finds that foot of day awake:
> Night-honey's there for bees to take.

But satire is another thing. Self-consciousness does tend to make satire less than convincing. Miss Sitwell does not seem to have written much verse that is, for the reader, primarily satirical, but Mr. Sacheverell Sitwell has written some and Mr. Osbert Sitwell has written some . . . and on what subjects! Democracy, rich men, bishops, the makers of wars, church-parades. Satire on a church-parade is merely an intellectual class-war. Why it is particularly stupid or wicked to wander by the sea with one's friends

THE SITWELLS 189

between a traditional religious ceremonial and the inevitable desirability of food, is extraordinarily difficult to understand. Nobody can imagine, surely, that (on the hypothesis of any bearable deity) *Before the Bombardment* or *Baroque Art* are much more important or satisfying than these other activities. More convenient to us, perhaps, because they suit our minds better, but what ice does our convenience cut? what frozen world of reality can we enter on it more than our fellow men?

Besides the fact that these satires are mostly aimed at things which it requires no particular courage to attack, and that many of them are based upon a false doctrine of relativity, there is also the fact that most of them are too long. Attack in verse is nearly always effective in proportion to its brevity. Even Pope's supreme efforts are short, and what better has there been since Pope than Shelley's two lines

> I met Murder on the way;
> He had a mask like Castlereagh,

or Mrs. Browning's single

> And kings crept out again to feel the sun?

This is why the most effective phrase in all this satire is Miss Sitwell's Bishop (the poor Bishops!) when he says

> There still remains Eternity
> (Swelling the diocese).

Apart from this (and Mr. Osbert Sitwell's happy success called *Sheep Song*), there is little in the satires except a proof that these distinguished and aristocratic writers have hearts that beat with their 'even

Christians'. They dislike people who cannot make up their own minds, but what a small fraction of a mind can anybody make up, and how certain he is to be wrong when he has done it!

More delightful are Osbert Sitwell's poems in *England Reclaimed*, his latest and best book. It is to be the first of a trilogy, and consists of a number of pieces presenting the housekeeper at the Great House, the servants, and the persons of the village. As, for example,

> Turning in, under the arches of the elder-bushes,
> With their rank, deserted smell,
> One would find Mr. Goodbeare,
> Surrounded by metallic music—
> Music of wood and steel—
> The central figure of his own
> Ballet Mécanique;
> Saw, plane and chisel
> Ground their various teeth and molars
> Loudly, ferociously,
> While he accompanied them
> With indicative gesture
> And appropriate word—
> For Mr. Goodbeare was attached
> To every kind of saw,
> Verbal or material,
> Was fond of proverbs and the Bible.

This 'broad panorama' 'essentially English' (and none the less so for being dated from Granada and Syracuse) is slipping, Mr. Sitwell says, 'by force of circumstances, into the past'. It may be so; if so, it is good to have such a presentation of it. Yet even here there is a faint suggestion of the superior intellect observing the inferior. 'Mrs. Southern' liked

A picture of a butcher's shop
        Just like a butcher's shop;

and

marble dimples in a marble baby's knuckle
        Just like the dimples in a baby's knuckle.

But there Mr. Sitwell stops, and does not pursue to its end the track through that other and equal being which opens from such words. All intellect, all imagination, is of course on his side in the quarrel, but as one reads one is provoked to shout, in a clamour of insane defiance, 'And a very good thing too! Cheers for Mrs. Southern!'

But the book establishes Mr. Osbert's place in the trio. (It is in mere reaction towards Mrs. Southern that one wants to call him Mr. Osbert, as if to be ranked willingly in that hierarchy of gardeners and kitchen-maids and villagers upon whom his observant and semi-sympathetic eyes look down.) Of all three worlds, his—it is clear from his other poems also—is that most near the workaday world. His poetic baby's knuckles are most like a baby's knuckles. His butcher's shop is most like a butcher's shop. This reclamation of England is from without certainly, but it is none the less beautiful and moving.

> Do you remember Mr. Goodbeare,
> Mr. Goodbeare who never forgot?
> Do you remember Mr. Goodbeare,
> That wrinkled and golden apricot,
> Dear, bearded, godfearing Mr. Goodbeare
> Who remembered remembering such a lot?

> Oh, do you remember, do you remember,
> As *I* remember and deplore,
> That day in drear and far-away December
> When dear, godfearing, bearded Mr. Goodbeare
> Could remember
> No more?

Between *England Reclaimed* and *The Hundred and One Harlequins* and *The Sleeping Beauty* it must be individual preference that chooses. In the last resort, in poetry, even the Sitwell family (it is at once sad and pleasing to think) are driven back on some such dogma as 'I don't know much about it, but I know what I like': who does know much about poetry?

Whichever one prefers (and one reader very definitely prefers *The Sleeping Beauty*—plus *Bucolic Comedies* and *Troy Park*), this group of writers are, and have always insisted on behaving as, a union, if not a unity. Admirable and moving poems, insane delights, thrilling voids, excitements, puzzles, laments, and lovelinesses—were there once wars among critics over these things? Can active and intelligent minds have annoyed other active and intelligent minds? It seems they did; fortunately it was all very long ago, and we need not worry. If it happened it was, however bitter, a shadow-conflict, much less real than the world in which 'Dagobert and Peregrine and I' walked by the sea, and, like the courageous children we all are when it is a question of Beauty,

> under the shelter of its lion voice
> proclaimed the name of Beauty, made our choice!

The darlings! But in the same poem, the introduction to *England Reclaimed*, Dagobert spoke of his sister as an 'ascetic artist', and the words, for all three, do not seem to be far wrong.

End Piece

Far away and very little
'mid pagodas rich and brittle
    pattered China's antique master;
round, below him, and above,
at the gate of a dark grove,
formal shapes began to move
    in a pattern of disaster.

There the Major and his lady
came from paths of hawthorn shady
    silhouetted on the walling
of an ancient country park,
where ran childhood, with the lark
singing, mingling with the dark
    that itself was softly calling.

There the darkness broke asunder
to interstices of wonder,
    wherethrough beauty glimmered grieving:
there a high fantastic march
issued through a dragon arch
overslept by elm and larch,
    where the Countess stood, receiving.

And the Countess sighed and muttered
and the Major sadly uttered
    what the Emperor was saying;
what the English Muse has said
since she lifted up her head
and the name of Chaucer read
    goes that newer music playing.

ROBERT GRAVES

Born in 1895. A son of Alfred Perceval Graves, a distinguished figure in the Irish literary movement. He served in France with Royal Welch Fusiliers, becoming known in England meanwhile as one of a group of three poets and friends; the others were Mr. Robert Nichols and Mr. Siegfried Sassoon. He was appointed Professor of English Literature, Egyptian University, in 1926.

His prose books have been mostly critical; among his books of poems are *Over the Brazier* (1916), *Fairies and Fusiliers* (1917), *Country Sentiment* (1920), *The Pier Glass* (1921), *Whipperginny* (1922), *The Feather Bed* (1923), *Mock Beggar Hall* (1924), *Welchman's Hose* (1925), and *Poems (1914–27)* (1927.)

THE greatest tribute that can be paid to Mr. Graves is to say how difficult it is, once his book is put down, not to copy him or to wish to do so. Others are for admiration and memory, but he is for imitation. It would not be surprising if this poet were driven to address, after the manner of Tennyson and Mr. Yeats, a more or less scornful remonstrance to 'certain bad poets, imitators of mine'. This is the more likely because Mr. Graves has something of hardness in his voice occasionally, both in his verse and when, for example, he launched an attack upon anthologies and an appeal to his fellow poets not to allow themselves to be represented in such things.

In the *Poems (1914–26)*, which he issued in 1927, he collected what are presumably the most important poems out of nine earlier thin volumes, not without a kick at certain of the omitted poems as 'merely "anthology pieces"'. These poems are divided into five books 'each distinct in character though un-labelled'. So un-Wordsworthian are Mr. Graves's own section-titles that (with one exception, 'War Poems') all the books are distinguished by the heading—

'Mainly such-and-such a date'. His publishers, not, it is to be hoped, entirely without his consent, went a little farther and on the inside of the book's jacket said, 'The poems are in five distinct phases: War Poems; Poems mostly fanciful and amatory; Poems of unrest; Metaphysical Poems; and Recent Poems which derive from, but do not repeat, what went before'. Any one who has read the book, though recognizing the goodwill of this attempt, will admit that it is unsatisfactory. Amatory is a horrid word; unrest is quite insufficient for the effect of certain poems; and the final phrase does not much help us. War is obvious; so is Metaphysical. The reader returns to Mr. Graves's own severity with a renewed conviction that poetry is not really much helped by these divisional headings.

Even fanciful? It seems almost ungrateful to call the earliest group of poems (mainly 1914–20) fanciful—especially when Mr. Graves has himself provided in a later poem so admirable a phrase for them—'my early sweetnesses' (if indeed he means the poems by it; we have to insert, with these modern obscurities, some such apologetic phrase). It is true he causes himself to be called 'fanciful spirit' in the preceding line; but 'fanciful spirit' in a poem sounds quite different from 'Poems fanciful and . . . ' in an announcement, so much are we still under the influence of the environment in which a word appears. But no more charming and accurate phrase could be found than 'early sweetnesses'; it is as exquisite as the poems themselves. And in themselves they illustrate the traditionalism and the newness of Mr. Graves's poetry. For they, or at any rate some of the best, are about nursery rhymes and fairy tales—and what could be more traditional? And they play with them complexly; they imagine new things about and for these old imaginings, and the new and the old dance happily together.

> But may the gift of heavenly peace
>   And glory for all time
> Keep the boy Tom who tending geese
>   First made the nursery rhyme.

And alongside this admirable and fabulous Tom go the equally admirable and presumably actual Davey and Jenny of the poem *A Song for Two Children*, of whose four stanzas the two middle ones may be quoted:

> Is there any song sweet enough
>   For Davey and for Jenny?
> Said Simple Simon to the pieman,
>   'Indeed, I know not any.
>
> 'I've counted the miles to Babylon,
>   I've flown the earth like a bird,
> I've ridden cock-horse to Banbury Cross,
>   But no such song have I heard.'

This is the old and the new in perfect harmony, poetry no less perfect that it is (in a sense) on a small scale: with how many solemn efforts at epic would we not buy it, and how unbuyable it is! But then the very first two poems of the section, and of the book, taught the true doctrine. The first is on *The Poet in the Nursery*, where 'the youngest poet' finds a book

> full of funny muddling mazes,
>   Each rounded off into a lovely song,
> And most extraordinary and monstrous phrases,
>   Knotted with rhymes like a slave-driver's thong,

And metre twisted like a chain of daisies
With great big splendid words a sentence long.

The line 'most extraordinary and monstrous phrases' could hardly be better exemplified than by the one that follows it, and again this union of the teaching of what ought to be done and the being able immediately to do it causes a new and remarkable delight. Nor will any one who receives satisfaction from those great lists of names which all the great poets have loved underrate the truth of the phrase in the next stanza, which speaks of 'learning the lines which seem to sound most grand'.

The second poem, *In the Wilderness*, is on the Temptation of Christ—again a theme sufficiently traditional. But it is exalted above the usual level, even of good verse on the subject, by its peculiar lucidity and pathos. Christ is seen speaking 'soft words of grace' to the 'desert-folk'—the bitterns, the 'she-pelican of lonely piety', 'basilisk, cockatrice', and at the end—with one of those sudden intensifications of which poetry is so full—it is told how there goes with Him

> Of all his wanderings
> Comrade, with ragged coat,
> Gaunt ribs—poor innocent—
> Bleeding foot, burning throat,
> The guileless old scapegoat.

There is no need to see in this (and some of Mr. Graves's later poems would anyhow prevent us doing so) any theological connexion. What makes the poem so moving is simply the picture of the lonely animal in that gentle company, the propinquity of the two wanderers, the unexpected association of the two traditions in a blessed enchantment—in short, the *poetry* of the thing. Has any poet or painter done it before Mr. Graves? And yet it is so obvious, once done. Dr. Watson's continual cry to Mr. Sherlock Holmes—'How simple!'—is our continual answer to much fine poetry (not, certainly, to all). Why *did* nobody think of it before? Why did no one think of the boy who made the first nursery rhyme? But no one did; according to the counsels of Eternity we had to wait for Mr. Graves.

This interlacing of old and new occurs, not only through the first section, but through all the *Poems*, but it is perhaps peculiarly striking in the first section. There are songs, and ballads (or poems in ballad style), and poems on an inn-sign and a thunderstorm and a glow-worm and a sewing-basket, and not one without some peculiar felicity. These felicities are perhaps partly due—at least, their explicable part is due (their inexplicable is due simply to genius) —to a curious mingling of what would, in the old phraseology, have been called romance and realism. The book, however wonderful, in *The Poet and the Nursery*, takes 'intimate dark stains from my hot hand'; the scapegoat has 'gaunt ribs' and other harms; the children waking in a confusion of thunder and fantastic bedtime stories

> cannot guess, could not be told
> How soon comes careless day,
> With birds and dandelion gold,
> Wet grass, cool scents of May.

And when it is a question of expressing (what is already present) a state of mind rather than an

outward fact, it is done by the same realistic detail.
Of a vain man we are told

> He walked on stilts
> To be seen by the crowd;

and there are many other examples.

This capacity to express new and significant detail, and yet to keep detail in its place, has accompanied Mr. Graves throughout his work. It is, no doubt, the mark of most poets worth calling by the name, but what makes it so fascinating in this work is that the most ordinary and present-day details are used for the purpose. A poet who can talk of unicorns and the Holy Grail and

> That ancient toad who sits immured
> Within your hearth-stone, light-forsaken,

relates in another poem how as a child he heard Mozart and, being rapt into an ecstasy, knotted his handkerchief for evidence that that ecstasy at least had been, and twenty years after realized that Mozart himself, being in the same ecstasy,

> Had knotted up his broad silk handkerchief
> In common music, rippling flat and brief.

This is the entirely credible detail which persuades us that poetry is a perfectly normal state of being. But Mr. Graves (unlike Mr. Yeats, who, if one may say so with the utmost worship, has always been inclined to make rather a fuss of being a poet) has been able to live at once in a poetic rage and in a poetic commonplaceness. There are a number of poems on poetry, expressing certainly different moods, of excitement and hope and doubt and depression; in one of the finest of which he speaks of it as simply as Shakespeare might.

> Poetry is, I said, my father's trade,
> Familiar since my childhood ...

and rejects all that solemn assumption of a dreadful destiny which, to name only dead poets, Shelley and Francis Thompson were inclined to make. It would be untrue to say that he approaches poetry from the side of prose (and certainly impossible for him to do so), but we may perhaps risk saying that he approaches it from the side of the world, in which nursery-rhymes and inn-signs and sewing-baskets play so fine a part. He does not, that is to say, merely make use of these admirable things to write poetry about, to decorate with fancies, to ornament with meditations; his poetry emerges from them, and, however we may remember them for the poetry, it is certainly the real things which we remember. The outer world moves with poetry and simply and naturally so.

Not that all Mr. Graves's poetry is simple, any more than the movement of the world is. There are poems which seem difficult probably because we have not yet sufficiently caught his own particular accent; and others which no proper humility need prevent us from protesting are difficult. There are a few, a very few, poems which become too metaphysical in the ordinary and not the poetic sense; and perhaps one or two which, in their too successful endeavour to speak in that subdued tone which is one of the achievements of modern verse—Edward Thomas did it to admiration—subdue themselves a little too much.

But excluding these, and it is little enough to exclude, we are still left a number of poems which deal with complicated matters and are themselves complicated, and some which, dealing with complicated matters, are themselves simple. And the finest of these are examples of how impossible it is to re-word in prose a subject which has been expressed in verse, except in a long and wearing treatise. In a poem called *The Avengers* Mr. Graves asks

> Who grafted quince on Western May?
> Sharon's mild rose on Northern briar?
> In loathing since that Gospel day
> The two saps flame, the tree's on fire.

There are only five more stanzas, and yet the effort (desirable or disastrous) to graft upon Europe, especially northern Europe, a tradition from the East has never been better expressed. 'Our wood leaps maddened ever since.'

> Crusading ivy Southward breaks
> And sucks your lordly palms upon,
> Our island oak the water takes
> To war with cedared Lebanon.

The rhythm, the adjectives, the meaning, are all so simple and so moving, and the meaning strikes at so deep a possibility, that one can only say 'What good poetry!' and leave it there.

> For bloom of quince yet caps the may,
> The briar is held by Sharon's rose,
> Monsters of thought through earth we stray,
> And how remission comes, God knows.

'Monsters of thought' is too huge a phrase for this poet's work, whether it be lyrical, narrative, or satiric, but there is a certain subdued monstrosity about it, which suggests itself in many different ways and shapes. There is no section of the *Poems* in which it is not felt. There are the frank monsters of the 'fanciful' poems—the basilisk and cockatrice—and in *An English Wood*, spoken of as being not there but somewhere else, harpies, gryphons, the roc, a mount of glass, and in other pleasant and monstrous fairy-tales

> How the Emperor's elder daughter
>   Fell in love with Will,
> And went with him to the Court of Venus
>   Over Hoo Hill.

These 'calm elementals' undergo many changes as the book proceeds, as it proceeds to take in more bitter experience and more creative ideas, but from the *War Poems* to *The Marmosite's Miscellany* imagined and romantic shapes appear. One of the best war poems that has been written is called *Dead Cow Farm*, and may be quoted in full:

> An ancient saga tells us how
> In the beginning the First Cow
> (For nothing living yet had birth
> But elemental Cow on Earth)
> Began to lick cold stones and mud:
> Under her warm tongue flesh and blood
> Blossomed, a miracle to believe,
> And so was Adam born, and Eve.
> Here now is chaos once again.
> Primaeval mud, cold stones and rain.
> Here flesh decays, and blood drips red,
> And the Cow's dead, the old Cow's dead.

If the ironic desolation has anywhere been better

expressed—but of course it has not. And this ironic monstrosity recurs again in that poem on the death of a friend which is called *Goliath and David* and tells how

> the historian of that fight
> Had not the heart to tell it right;

the real truth that Goliath 'steel-helmeted and grey and grim' killed David. Such a reversal of antique story is in the modern mode; the most notorious example is Rupert Brooke's sonnet on Helen. But this poem is so much the better than that as its passion is intense and its irony derived from its passion, instead of merely being picked up at random and being therefore a little cheap. All through the *War Poems* the emotions expressed in two separate lines— 'the Cow's dead, the old Cow's dead', and 'Shame for beauty's overthrow!' cross and recross each other.

And in the next section ('mainly 1920–3') which is called by the publishers 'poems of unrest'— although at certain moments 'poems of nightmare' would seem a better title—these two notes go sounding on. 'Beauty's overthrow' may sometimes be beauty's triumph; that is a matter of small moment—what is important is the traditional and increasingly metaphysical sense of beauty expressed. But here also fabulous monsters still move; here are the Unicorn and the White Doe, mermaids and dragons, witch and incubus. Nevertheless, there is here a growing sense that these poems, with their imagery, are striving towards their central subject. Beautiful or nightmarish, tale or song, the poetry is concentrating on something, and that something is the nature of man and the universe. But its concentration is according to the nature of Mr. Graves's own mind, and therefore it is allusive, symbolical, rich with a sense of its own being rather than with the expression of it. Though Mr. Graves can be lucid enough, and at times satiric, he does not seem to be by nature epigrammatic. The tales and the songs even are put there to show us the world, and if they do it is rather the inner world of man's mind than the outer that they suggest. So when we come to the metaphysical poems ('mainly 1923–5') it is still rather the stories and comments than the directly philosophic verses which seem the most pleasant.

Here is the poem called *The Avengers*, which was quoted earlier; and here a very remarkable poem—one of the best that Mr. Graves has given us—called *The Clipped Stater*. More even than with most poems it is impossible to extract anything that can reasonably be called its 'meaning' from it; it is a fable of the deified Alexander the Great, who, supposed to be dead, is serving in the frontier-guard of 'a land of yellow men', and how one day there comes to him in his pay

> a Silver Alexander
> Coined from the bullion taken at Arbela. . . .
> But he cannot fathom what the event may mean.
> Was his lost Empire, then, not all-embracing?
> And how does the stater, though defaced, owe service
> To a God that is as if he had never been?

The impression this poem leaves is out of proportion to anything it metaphysically says—which is why it may be called a good poem: the strange country, the frontier-post, the 'feast of fish and almonds', and the greying figure of Alexander, once a god, are the things that persuade us to accept it. It seems here as if the two manners, or modes of thought, in which Mr. Graves has indulged, had come together and made a third. Alexander and the Djinn are there—fairy-tales; and the realistic details —'and he grows grey and eats his frugal rice'; and metaphysics—'whether God can be by his own confines accursèd?' But the effect is none of these singly; it is as if consideration of man's mind and the nature of things had almost begun to shape itself in a new myth.

In a satire, which there is no room here to discuss, called the *Marmosite's Miscellany*, Mr. Graves has said

> The beginning of wisdom is laughter and song,
> The furtherance of wisdom, scholarship and groans.
> Between first and second reactions are strong;
> The disputants wrangle in no playful tones,
> Dream against waking, blood against bones:
> Let poetry, then, enter on its third degree,
> In grammar of unreason marching close and free.

As in *The Poet in the Nursery*, so in this poem Mr. Graves is doing what he teaches. It is because his poetry seems to be 'in grammar of unreason marching close and free' that he is, in the dull phrase with which it is a pleasure to mock him, 'one of the most interesting of the younger established poets'.

End Piece

End Piece

Sing a song of sixpence!
   What do poets buy?
Unicorns and zebras
   and hippopotami,
jungle-huts and garden-walks,
   stories never told,
stories told a thousand times,
   and words new and old.

Sing a song of sixpence!
   What do poets buy?
Hy-Brasil and Valhalla
   and the Erymanthian sty.
Bucephalus and Pegasus
   and chargers many more,
and metaphysic subtleties
   and philosophic lore.

Sing a song of sixpence!
   What do poets buy?
Five-pennyworth of knowledge
   whereof the pedants lie,
of birds and morns and music
   and gospels far-renowned;
one-pennyworth of something else
   the world has never found.

EDMUND BLUNDEN

Born in 1896. During the war he served with the Royal Sussex; afterwards he became sub-editor of the (then separate) *Athenaeum*, and contributor to the literary papers. *The Waggoner*, 1920, was followed by *The Shepherd*, 1922, for which he received the Hawthornden Prize. From 1924-7 he was Professor of English Literature at Tokio University. His other books of verse are *To Nature*, 1923; *Masks of Time*, 1925; *English Poems*, 1925; *Retreat*, 1928; *Near and Far*, 1929. He is an authority on the literary history of the early part of the nineteenth century, and has written one of the best books on the war—*Undertones of War*, 1928.

IT has been said, and not wholly unjustly, that the younger contemporary poets have only one fault—dullness. Observation, dexterity, feeling, they have, but between their experience and their expression the interest has slipped away. They tell us of their imaginations and we do not care to know; they are sincere, but their sincerity is of no importance, or they are insincere and we are not excited enough to protest. The English Muse has known times of mediocrity before now, but this is a mediocrity of a different kind. These modern poems do not come from a corrupt following of some dying school; they have not lost originality or grace or charm or knowledge. They are good poems, they are all but poetry, yet the final felicity is somehow withheld. Sometimes it seems as if this were due to a lack of poetic intellect; the epigram in a line or a couplet which is so characteristic of all the greater and many of the lesser poets is almost wholly absent. These poets have as much of our ordinary working-day brains as the rest of us; their meditations are as subtle, their philosophies no less, but no more, surely based—they remark what we do and turn it into rhythm. But the faculty of compressing such meaning into a phrase is denied to them. We have to cover as much ground in their verse as in our own thoughts, and consequently we tire as soon.

To say that the distinguishing mark of Mr. Blunden's Muse is that she tires with us would be to offer him a doubtful phrase; so would the suggestion that he has made this dullness interesting. But, obliquely, such a dullness does seem to be his subject —not the lack of intellect, but the lack of interest. And before pursuing this inquiry it should be noted that in fact Mr. Blunden *has* written one of the few compressed and greatly poetic lines of contemporary verse. Few reviewers can have done a greater service to literature than Mr. J. C. Squire when, in a review of Mr. Blunden's *The Waggoner*, he quoted from the poem *Almswomen* 'All things they have in common, being so poor'. The line leapt to the eye as being at once in the grand style. Beyond the mere fact that it told, it had in itself a sense of depth and significance. It established itself permanently in the memory, and could be quoted, without indecency, in the presence of Shakespeare himself.

So high a triumph cannot often befall a poet unless he be one of the greater ones, which perhaps Mr. Blunden is; he has time and space before him to show. But having admired with all possible worship the achievement of such a line we may admit that it is exactly the largeness and the intensity of it which are lacking in many of our poets, and even (comparably anyhow) in Mr. Blunden himself. But he has one great advantage—he does not stress and accentuate his own personality. The 'I's of his poems are subdued; he is not his own centre. *He* is not dull, for he is so little there to be dull. His very style is as impersonal as can be, and perhaps this is what distinguishes it. There is in it a perpetual quiet, but it is a quiet which flows towards such profundities as are heard in the line already quoted. That line has in its particularity the general sense that Mr. Blunden's poems are in movement. They are not the contained wayside pools of much modern verse; they proceed towards infinity.

They proceed, however, through quite definite surroundings, natural, poetic, and spiritual. Some half of them (it is an impressionistic, not a statistical, reckoning) are concerned with the English landscape or English village life. Since Clare (to whom Mr. Blunden has addressed several poems and of whose own poems he has been a joint-editor) there has been —except for Edward Thomas—no such expanded and detailed sense of country life—plant and animal and man. Let the titles witness: *Sheepbells*, *The Pike*, *The Dried Millpond*, *Molecatcher*, *First Snow*, *The Poor Man's Pig*, and so on. They are the natural records of a natural life; they draw few morals and insist on none. In *Molecatcher*, for example, after the poem has described how the old man has gone the round of his snares, and left death 'smirking in the hole', it proceeds

> And moles to him are only moles; but hares
> See him afield and scarcely cease to nip
> Their dinners, for he harms not them; he spares
> The drowning fly that of his ale would sip
> And throws the ant the crumbs of comradeship.
> And every time he comes into his yard

> Grey linnet knows he brings the groundsel sheaf
> And clatters round the cage to be unbarred
> And on his finger whistles twice as hard.—

This is how things are. Moles are slain and other things treated courteously. But there is no bitterness or irony; none but a humanitarian hot-gospeller could press Mr. Blunden into service. It is precisely one of his virtues that he does not fidget us with his opinions or even demand that we should form opinions of our own; we are concerned with such things in his verse in quite another way.

It is a way which, nevertheless, has its limitations, or at least its definitions. There is communicated in these poems no ecstasy and little joy; the steady, slow, universal life which they record discovers no such raptures. There is an occasional—and very beautiful—poem of fantasy, but Mr. Blunden's verse hardly ever moves rapidly. His thunderstorms are equable and his north winds restrained. Extreme freshness and extreme roughness are alien to his mind; they dwell in a world of more immediate apprehension than Mr. Blunden normally inhabits, in the world (perhaps) of childhood. There are poems about childhood, but it is childhood at a distance. Distance is in this poetry, and a knowledge of the grave weariness that came in traversing that distance. Such weariness has certainly not affected the stanzas, nor does it affect the reader, but it is in many places their unacknowledged subject. The mere mass of details accentuate it; they are all comments on the single Shakespearian line 'A long while ago the world began'. The rustics are old, the shepherd, the molecatcher, the almswomen, the matmender, the gipsy wives, and others—they have travelled far in time. And other experiences which are the subjects of poems are such as in themselves cause memories of the passage of many years—war and death.

Mr. Blunden's war poems have their own peculiar truth, and more truth than many others. They are, most of them, written as memories, but the memory is not 'in tranquillity'; it is wounded and suffering with the hurt it bears in mind. It is like a man waking out of sleep, long before dawn, to remember a nightmare, who is yet encircled by the night. The nightmare itself is broken, yet the conditions out of which it came are still there, and his relief is haunted by the insecurity of his accustomed surroundings.

> Swift away the century flies,
>   Time has yet the wind for wings,
> In the past the midnight lies,
>   But my morning never springs.
>
> And still you mutter wandering on
> Over the shades of shadows gone.

There is one poem, *The Avenue*, which describes the poet walking up a 'long colonnade' of trees, and suddenly losing his interest in their individuality because in the mere number of them he finds himself again tramping with his men up the line, and the lights over it—

> plucking at Death's sleeve
> They showed him in the nick new skulls to cleave.

The poem ends

> Now on the sky I see the dull lights burn
> Of that small village whither I return.

> The trees hide backward in the mists, the men
> Are lying in their thankless graves agen,
> And I a stranger in my home pass by
> To seek and serve the beauty that must die.

The very next poem is called *Reunion in War*, and speaks of a lover returning by night to his 'more than dear'—

> O cruel time to take away,
>   And worse to bring agen;
> Why slept not I in Flanders clay
>   With all the murdered men?
>
> For I had changed, or she had changed,
>   Though true loves both had been,
> Even while we kissed we stood estranged
>   With the ghosts of war between.
>
> We had not met but a moment ere
>   War baffled joy, and cried,
> 'Love's but a madness, a burnt flare;
>   The shell's a madman's bride'.

Another poem begins

> Tired with dull grief, grown old before my day,

and speaks of the poet as 'dead as the men I loved'. There is to be felt in them all a weariness almost beyond cure, a horror of which the chief horror is that it is not unendurable. War takes away something from the spirit and leaves the combatant

> Having no part in common day or joy.

It is because common day and common joy have been the subjects of so much meditation in other verses that their lack here is so poignant.

> All things they have in common, being so poor.
>
> Having no part in common day or joy.

The large intensity which makes 'common' so beautiful a word in the first line is the measure of the loss expressed in the second use. The mad war has taken away that universal thing, has hidden, if not destroyed, 'the human heart by which we live'. Friendships are perished; friends are dead. 'Necromantic thought' alone can reunite them in memory of the lines and 'half-stricken towers'. In one poem a spirit from heaven
goes abroad attuned

to this wild mood and hears it from all sides. The chaos of *Third Ypres* was terrible enough when it was chaos in which the army strove.

> Still wept the rain, roared guns,
> Still swooped into the swamps of flesh and blood
> All to the drabness of uncreation sunk,
> And all thought dwindled to a moan,—Relieve!
> But who with what command can now relieve
> The dead men from that chaos, or my soul?

Not general death only, but individual, haunts this verse. There are several poems on the death of a child, and the contrast between the immortality of that childhood and the mortal maturity of the poet does but seem to increase the sense of distance which in so many ways offers itself. This is none the less so that no mere sentimentality is allowed to enter. One poem reminds the reader of Wordsworth's *The Fountain*:

I came to the churchyard where pretty Joy lies
   On a morning in April, a rare sunny day;
Such bloom rose around, and so many bird's cries,
   That I sang for delight as I followed the way.

I sang for delight in the ripening of spring,
  For dandelions even were suns come to earth;
Not a moment went by but a new lark took wing
  To wait on the season with melody's mirth.

. . . .

This peace, then, and happiness thronged me around.
  Nor could I go burdened with grief, but made merry,
Till I came to the gate of that overgrown ground
  Where scarce once a year sees the priest come to bury.

This is how things are; and in another poem is the realization that

> though one of those dear blooms
> Fall, still great childhood lords it all the way,
> And the whole earth may see and hear and glory.

The poems of such a reconciliation are no less convincing than the poems of sadness. But this is a natural sorrow and a natural healing—so far as such sorrow is healed,—and is different from the hard exhaustion of the war poems. Only, if Time and Nature heal, their method is slow, and if not weariness at least endurance and change are implied.

This poet's kinship with John Clare has been mentioned, but there are older poets than Clare to whom he has been devoted, and one of them is Henry Vaughan. Mr. Blunden has published an 'essay' on him with translations of the Latin Poems. He has written in one book a poem on *The Age of Herbert and Vaughan*, and another, *A Psalm*, ends

> O God that Abraham and our Vaughan knew,
> Hide not thyself, let first love prove not wrong.

None of Mr. Blunden's poems are more admirably right than this. The poem seems indeed like a transcription in verse of some psalm; its sadness is the movement of David's song (the ascription is in the verse), and yet its hope and delight and refuge come from David through Vaughan and his peers. It could not have been written by Vaughan, but it has been written by a descendant of Vaughan's with a less simple genius. Its mildness and patience do not prevent it being passionate, and direct passion is as a rule a little lacking in this verse. That it is there is obvious; if it were not, the verse would not be nearly as good as it is. No poet can write verse without passion, but those whose passion seeks to become one with the movement of the earth, the growth of flowers, the flow of the country stream, and the steady repetition of day and night, have set out on a longer journey than many others, and the sense of that distance again is in these poems. Vaughan desired to run after his childhood and longed to repossess it; in a later age of verse Mr. Blunden meditates on it and on 'the Death of Childhood Beliefs'.

> How shall I return and how
>   Look once more on those old places!
> For Time's cloud is on me now
>   That each day, each hour, effaces
>   Visions once on every bough.

One would like to see Mr. Blunden involved in a newspaper controversy with some infidel who denied Vaughan's genius or Clare's, rather with a feeling that the wrath of the Lamb might be, as Mr. Chesterton has asserted, the most terrible of all. His remonstrance with Shakespeare on behalf of the primrose, whom the earlier poet most unfairly coupled

with libertinage and hell, is charmingly beautiful and
restrained. And as one turns the pages of his books
and reads so many lovely descriptions, so many
poignant sympathies, such definite endurances and
pains, such goodwill towards joy, it is clearer than
before that the dullness which Mr. Blunden has
made interesting is not that of a striving talent but
the dullness common to us all. Slowly the monotony
of the passage of Time presents itself here as a slow
and lovely thing; it, or Mr. Blunden's verse, subdues
us to itself. And then with hardly a change of voice—
only sinking a little as Wordsworth would do—from
admirable work to supreme perfection—that verse
goes on to say how two old women lived together:

> All things they have in common, being so poor.

End Piece

A lantern passes down the path—and there
    one goes: who? Herbert, that young star turned saint?
Or the less-nurtured poet of hedgerows, Clare?
    or but some Farmer's Boy? The step grows faint.

Night and the knowledge of the place come down;
    the pool there; there the farm; over the hill
the high road—Fancy fleeing from the town
    comes back to the village, fain to dwell there still;

there the first primrose; there the fairy-round;
    there the thronged churchyard where so many suns
descend to sleep: nay there—what light, what sound?
    the lights above the lines; the sound of the guns.

www.ingramcontent.com/pod-product-compliance
Lightning Source LLC
Chambersburg PA
CBHW022058160426
43198CB00008B/278